WALES ON THE WIRELESS

Wales on the Wireless

A Broadcasting Anthology

edited by
PATRICK HANNAN

in association with

First Impression — 1988

ISBN 0 86383 447 7

Printed by
J. D. Lewis & Sons Ltd., Gomer Press, Llandysul, Dyfed

ACKNOWLEDGEMENTS

There is a great deal of fascinating material in the BBC's Welsh archive. I have been very fortunate in the people who have helped me dig out some of the best of it and put it into this present shape. It was Keith Davies who took the initial plunge into back numbers of *Radio Times*, followed by an invaluable assessment of thousands of pages of script. In turn that was made possible by the patience and expertise of Ann Goddard and the rest of the staff of the BBC Registry in Cardiff. What they could not discover came largely from the sound archives, where Iris Cobbe was able to make sense of definitive requests like: "I'm sure he did a programme sometime in the sixties." She was strongly backed by specific contributions from John Ormond, Elwyn Evans, Mark Owen and Herbert Williams, among others. Those who promised to help but didn't can remain in decent obscurity. Not for the first time, Gill Robbins achieved the near-impossible, not only by typing the original text, but by seeing to it that the raw materials did not get seriously disorganised, never mind lost. Dai Smith read the manuscript and made a lot of helpful suggestions. He will be surprised to see that I have adopted a large number of them. My wife, Menna, also read the typescript and is responsible for many improvements of clarification, spelling, punctuation and style. She also undertook the even more difficult task of listening to me going on about the project over many months. John and Huw Lewis of Gomer Press remained calm throughout (up to the time of writing, anyway) and saw to it that the original idea became paper and ink. Finally, of course, I must thank the broadcasters, who are acknowledged by their presence, but, above all, the producers who commissioned the original scripts and transmuted them into programmes. Their names are not included, but it is their work too that is largely celebrated.

INTRODUCTION

It is a curious thing that Wales, which has produced so many brilliant journalists, should itself be so lacking in journalism. Of course it has newspapers and broadcasting organisations, but that is not at all the same thing. As in other fields, it seems to have specialised in the export of talent: the Cudlipp brothers, for instance, each of whom became a Fleet Street editor and one of whom, Hugh, ended up running a huge press empire. Then there were the Berry brothers from Merthyr Tydfil, three of whom became peers, including the newspaper tycoons Kemsley and Camrose. Today the national newspapers, radio and television are full of the work of dozens who—Welsh or not—honed their talents in the unkempt newsroom of Thomson House, Cardiff.

Wales clearly isn't deficient in ability, but in what you might call a journalistic constituency. Naturally you can find out about strikes and murders, about who made what speech, who's gone bankrupt, who scored the winning try and all that sort of thing. What is less easy to discover is thoughtful analysis of events and movements, attempts to answer questions about why Wales is like it is, whether it should change and, if so, how.

So, for example, there is scarcely any informed criticism of broadcasting—come to that, not much of any kind. What we learn of politics often reflects the worst tendencies of Parliament itself—an unenlightening and mindless yah-booism occasionally spiced up with a little gossip. Literary criticism is largely confined to periodicals which are not what you might call—well—terribly *accessible*. And in all these matters there is often a tremendous leaden earnestness; fun is usually the first thing to be squeezed out when we put Welsh public life through the journalistic mangle.

Oddly enough, though, this applies much more forcefully to contemporary matters than it does to the past.

Nothing in recent years has flourished with quite the same vigour as has the study of Welsh history. Books pour from academics like sweat in a turkish bath, analysing in particular the Welsh condition in the nineteenth and twentieth centuries and, by implication, that of today.

They've attacked this rich seam like demented colliers, indiscriminately winding to the surface tram-loads of prose ranging from the incandescent to the incomprehensible. A few years ago, even, there were two television histories of Wales running more or less simultaneously on the UK networks. What the rest of Britain made of this is not recorded.

But this outburst of energy, this appetite for self-examination discovered by the historians, is not reflected very widely in Welsh journalism. One obvious reason is the lack of appropriate institutions. Only the BBC and HTV can seriously claim to provide a service on a Welsh national basis. The *Western Mail* and the *Daily Post* in effect divide the Welsh morning newspaper circulation geographically between them. Magazines and other publications, such as they are, tend to squeak only briefly before being caught in the trap of no money and no readers. Whether all this is symptom or a cause is, however, difficult to say.

But in any case, proprietors of newspapers and people who run broadcasting stations would argue that their main job is to attract customers—paying or otherwise—through providing information and entertainment, the two great crowd-pullers. Neither group would concede that their principal role should be to conduct some kind of extended seminar on Welsh life. In addition they would insist that they are anyway fulfilling this function. Programmes and articles do examine Welsh concerns with insight, intelligence and care. Those historians, for instance, can be seen and read all over the place.

Nevertheless, what I believe this anthology shows is that we could do with more of it; that the need and the capacity to fulfill it are demonstrated by the contribution made to broadcasting over more than fifty years by the most accomplished writers, academics and commentators. They have illuminated the continuing debate about what kind of place Wales is and should be. They have done so because they've been asked to do so. As the late Hywel Davies, a former BBC Wales Head of Programmes asserted: "Broadcasting people should march, most of the time, in the vanguard of their society."

This collection has come to be part of that argument largely by accident—or at least because of the nature of the material available. It is certainly idiosyncratic, perhaps eccentric and, I dare say, it will also prove irritating to some people. What it does, though, is illustrate what I mean by journalism.

Broadcasting is of course ephemeral, but that should be a matter for thanksgiving rather than regret. That's not because the natural home of much of it is the waste bin, but because being ephemeral is one of the things that defines broadcasting—if it all translated readily to the written word then it wouldn't have made very good listening.

In fact, since the BBC began its first service in Wales in 1923, the bulk of its raw material has been drawn from things like music, drama, sport, news and light entertainment—things that either cannot be read or which would be meaningless if reproduced here. For that reason the people who said to me, "You've got to have a bit of *Welsh Rarebit* in," are going to be disappointed, but not as disappointed as they would have been if they'd seen it, cold on the page. For similar reasons I've reluctantly put aside most of the radio features made by people like Elwyn Evans and the incredibly prolific Philip Burton. The life of those programmes is in hearing them.

Indeed, even some of those who care most passionately about both the written and the spoken word, people like Wynford Vaughan-Thomas and Gwyn Thomas, lose something when you cannot hear them—but there's plenty left and even on the page they remain vivid, passionate and compelling.

But some people are pure radio—like Alun Williams whose skills have adorned British broadcasting for something like forty years. His ease, his command, his fluency are remarkable but, like others, he is for listening to, not reading. Anyway, there are grave doubts as to whether such a thing as an Alun Williams *script* actually exists.

Nowadays techniques of recording and editing, of constructing programmes (or *not* constructing them, quite often) have become increasingly sophisticated and have therefore made radio more and more its own medium rather than an adaptation of another form—the theatre, say, or the lecture hall.

One man and his mike is an increasingly rare, anachronistic combination, largely replaced by one man and his turntable or one man and his telephone. It's no good complaining about it, any more than it is about the fact that announcers don't wear dinner jackets and that there's no longer a Home Service. The important question is whether the richness of ideas and argument contained in the BBC's Welsh archive can still find a place in Welsh journalism, even if it's in a new style.

Obviously the answer is yes—well, up to a point, anyway. In my opinion one of the best pieces in the entire collection was broadcast as recently as 1983. It's Alun Richards' obituary of Carwyn James and it's as stunning a combination of clear-sighted description and deeply-felt affection as you'll ever read.

But what's most astonishing in a search through the archives is the range and distinction of the people to whom the BBC in Wales acted as a clearly benevolent publisher. Writers like Dylan Thomas, Jack Jones, Dannie Abse and Idris Davies are there. Academics like Gwyn Jones (a writer as well, of course) and Brinley

Thomas were frequent contributors. Artists like John Petts and Josef Herman were heard, as were figures as diverse as Goronwy Rees, Thomas Jones and Arthur Horner.

Equally fascinating, though, are the unknown people whose stories were broadcast through series like *Where We Came From* during the Thirties. There is, for example, the remarkable history of Gebuza Nungu, the Zulu who became a Llanelli tinplate worker; or Antonio Leonardi who genuinely believed that gold could simply be picked up in the streets of Wales.

These broadcasts, and hundreds like them, add up to a revealing portrait of Wales since 1934. (Sadly, no material seems to survive between the start of broadcasting and that date.) The people who made them address important issues about language, culture, economics, literature, arts and history; they ask distinctive Welsh questions about these subjects.

They describe, too, and nowhere more movingly than in the opening sentences of Harry Soan's explanation of how he and his wife first came to Wales. "In the spring of 1932 our first child died. By the autumn we felt we had better go away and see if a change of scene would help change our frame of mind." A bitter family tragedy poignantly captured in a few dozen unadorned words.

There's much, as well, that's intriguing, nothing more so than Lord Tonypandy's encounter with Stalin. Who wouldn't have paid good money to be present at the meeting between the Rhondda chapel boy socialist and one of history's greatest mass murderers.

And it's a pleasure to read a noted Welsh language poet sparkling in English—T. Glynne Davies being bright and mischievous and ironical. The sad thing is that he died before he could complete his work on a selection of the best of Welsh-language broadcasting.

The penalty for such digging into the past is, naturally, acute nostalgia, the most obvious symptom of which is an unshakeable belief that things were once wonderful and that they are not half as good now. Nevertheless, I think this selection shows some of the range of inquiry, exposition and provocative consideration that's been available in Wales during the last fifty years or so. It's certainly possible to argue that there's no point in being Welsh broadcasters—or newspapermen come to that—if we don't make it part of our responsibility to continue this process of self-examination which is a crucial part of journalism.

Above all it would be a crime if, in another fifty years someone went to open the archive cupboard and found it was empty.

CONTENTS

INCIDENT IN A BOOKSHOP

RHYS DAVIES

I was browsing in a London bookshop recently and heard this remark from a lady, whom at first glance I should have judged to be intelligent. She was choosing a pile of novels to take with her to her country-house. She stared suspiciously at the jacket of a book which the assistant was recommending. "Oh, no, not this one," she exclaimed. "It's about Wales. I can't *bear* novels about Wales. They've nothing but rain and strikes and gloom down there." Glancing at her more attentively I saw then that she looked stupid really. I felt obliged to say loudly to the assistant, "I'll have that Welsh novel. They tell me it's a very fine piece of work." The book was one of my own.

But the Welsh took, take up a suspicious attitude towards novels about themselves. I am speaking now of novels which attempt to reproduce some honest picture of modern life in Wales. A writer will, of course, be forgiven if he will flatter and prettify. He must not talk about sex, and if he deals with religion, he must be pious. He must drown the lovely country cottages in roses, he must sentimentalize over the Welsh miners and rhapsodize over the farms and farmers, he must make the women dewy daisies, the men clean and wholesome as pats of fresh butter. The Welsh are not the only people who prefer this kind of romanticism. But I think we are unique in the wrath we display when writers dare to touch what some call, rhetorically, dirt, others truth. And we will not understand that a writer can be critical of the nation and still remain enamoured of it, that criticism does not always come out of sourness or hatred. Instead, with looks tall as a policeman's truncheon, we thrash the loving but unromantic writer out of the paradise of our land. I think the explanation of this display of wrath is that we imagine all other nations but ourselves are resplendent with all the virtues, that we alone are

1

addicted to the unpleasant behaviour which this writer-fellow has dared to reveal. In a word, our old friend inferiority complex is the moving force in this fury.

When I was last in a Welsh chapel, I was fascinated by a nose whose owner sat near me. It was a bulky nose, with personality, and it shone with the most magnificent tint of greenish-purple. That greenish-purple has been stored away in my memory ever since, attached to associative notes on the nose, the man, the chapel. As a writer I would some day like to use that tint, that nose, perhaps the man—though I may attach the nose to a woman, as opportunity presents. I probably will. But this does not mean the writer is implying that all people in Wales have bulky greenish-purple noses. Yet sure enough some day I shall receive a Welsh letter of protest, or someone will angrily tell me that he has lived in Wales all his life and never seen such a nose, that Welsh people are *not* greenish-purple in their faces. Just as every now and again they publicly protest that Welsh people do *not* do this, that, and the other; do *not* speak this way *or* that way, are not immoral and rascals, do not eat peas with a knife, do not go to bed in their day shirts; this book is not a *true* mirror of Welsh life, but a lot of perverted trash.

1938

TWO FACES FOR A WELSHMAN

JOHN MORGAN

The Welsh are a self-conscious people. Whether this is because Wales is a historically defeated nation, or because the omnipresence of mountains turns men in on themselves, or whether it is because the nonconformist gospel of a special providence with its message of individual dignity and personal value has dominated the life of peasant and industrial worker, I shouldn't like to say. But

2

I think they—we, that is—are given to self-analysis. We are all well acquainted with the idea of Wales and the kinds and conditions of its people. We are, more than most, accustomed to expatiating on our society and national character, both for the benefit of ourselves and particularly for that of visiting observers, whose gullibility we believe infinite.

When Englishmen are invited to offer observations on their national character—or indeed any other subject—they are often at a loss for words. We, taking our time, at length, will frankly confess to the virtues of idealism, integrity and godliness that we believe ourselves to possess. Without false modesty, we'll mention our gift of words, our talent for melodic harmony, our natural genius for the game of rugby football. Other countries may, from time to time, defeat us at football, but these are merely the triumphs of brute strength over talent. If the visiting observer is *au fait* with the fashionable sociological *argot*, we will be quick to note the classlessness of Welsh society, implying that this makes us healthier than the crowd across the dyke.

And then, making obeisance in passing to our sense of fair play, we will announce our shortcomings. That charm, for example, which too easily slips across the frontiers of hypocrisy. But why, our visiting observer will ask, getting a word in edgeways, are Welshmen all things to all people; why do they agree with one man, and then turn away and agree also with his enemy? This, our Welshman responds, is *not* being two-faced, but is the expression of our kind heart, our desire to hurt no-one's feelings. And then there is that sense of the theatrical, that yen for rhetoric which, alas, will frequently admire performance above content, and prefer the mask to the reality. There's that high incidence of miserliness in the less populated areas. But these Goriots of the high ground, one emphasises, represent that equally passionate obverse of our more general impulse to generosity.

Some of us, depending on the degree of sophistication or scepticism our positions in life permit us, will even touch on the famous Welsh alchemist act.

This, as we all know, is that contortion performed daily in towns and villages and newspapers up and down *yr hen wlad* in which base talent, provided it's local, is magically transformed into a golden boy. And then, to demonstrate for the visiting observer's benefit, our familiarity with the life cultural, whether acquired in college, workingman's institute or WEA class, will throw in lightly a maxim of, let's say, La Rochefoucauld's: "If we ever admit our shortcomings, it is through vanity." Now, a *Welsh* Rochefoucauld, we will add, would amend that maxim and say of his fellow-countrymen: "It is the particular vanity of the Welsh to be as proud of their failings as their virtues". At which the visiting observer will reel exhausted from the company of the self-analyst, a departure which our Welshman, now entranced by his own eloquence, will scarcely notice.

1961

A NEW LIFE

Kate Bosse-Griffiths

I used to be very shy to reveal the fact that I have had a prolonged University education. I kept in my mind the popular prejudice that a real woman should not be a 'blue-stocking' and that a girl who has the bad luck to be an 'intellectual' should at least try and hide it as well as possible. But even before I had time to settle down to married life my husband's family urged me on: "Surely you will give an address to our Young People's Society?" and they were even disappointed to find that I did not have a half a dozen public lectures ready for choice. A new life full of activities opened itself for me, quite different from the monotonous provincial life of which some friends had warned me. The Rhondda seemed to be teeming with societies, most of them connected with the non-conformist chapels which needed speakers to address them and chairmen to preside at their meetings; adult schools, sisterhoods, young people's societies, unemployed clubs: they sensed that I had something to offer them even before I had realised it myself.

The Welsh people did not patronise me as a foreigner, nor did they look down at me as one of those 'intellectuals,' but they made use of my gifts, they gave me opportunity to develop them through exercise and with that they made me feel that I am in my right place in life. I felt as if I had started a new life; and really, like a growing child I am now trying to master a new language—the Welsh language. I learn Welsh not only in order to get to know the riches of the Welsh literature, though that, as Dr. Bell's book on Welsh poetry shows, would be well worth while, but in order to come nearer to the soul of the Welsh, because they are proud people who know their own value and feel a delight in being discovered and appreciated. Every attempt of mine to express myself in Welsh was greeted with a smiling satisfaction which was already a reward of its own, and urged on through this smile I hastened to get over the stage when people stopped talking Welsh as soon as I entered the room and changed over to English, to show that they did not have any secrets in front of me.

1942

A PROPER NATION

Goronwy Rees

Until I was eighteen I suppose I had hardly ever left
Wales; and I remember that my strongest desire was to
leave it for what I imagined to be the less constricted, less
narrow, less puritanical life of other countries. Since then
I have not lived in Wales except for very brief periods. I
have lived in England and abroad, and I confess that by
now I am much fonder of my country than before; and
my people seem to me to possess more of those qualities I
admire, of passion, intelligence, individualism, and of
natural devotion to culture than almost any other I have
known.

I am speaking now of the ordinary working class
Welshman and not of the middle class. But at the same
time I feel that as a nation—and we are a nation in every
proper sense of the word—we suffer in all our affairs from
the curse of all small nations that have not got some great
mission to fulfil—that is the curse of being parochially and
provincially minded and of refusing to judge ourselves by
the highest European standards.

We claim to have exceptional talents but refuse to
accept the standards which every really exceptional
talent must submit to. With few exceptions our great
men enjoy purely local fame—or should I say notoriety. It
seems to me that precisely by urging the acceptance to
higher standards those who live outside Wales can do
most to help their country; but to do that they must first
test themselves, their manners, customs, ways of thought,
by those of other countries, especially those which have
contributed most in modern times to European civilisation.
Fortunately I believe that some such thing has already
begun to happen.

Let me take an example from that activity which
interests me most. Nothing gives me greater pleasure and
hope at the present moment than to know that there

exists in Wales a group of young writers, mostly writing in English, whose work, whatever its quality, can only be properly judged by the same standards which we apply to the writers of France or England or Spain. The best place to read their works is, I suppose, the excellent little magazine called *Wales* which is published and edited by Mr. Keidrych Rhys at Carmarthen. It amuses me to wonder whether the appearance of this magazine seems as important to those who live in Wales as to myself who does not. You may not like its verses and stories; what is important is that its contributors, while remaining Welsh in their inspiration, their way of writing and feeling, measure themselves by the standards which are common to all the literatures of Europe. There are other writers also like Mr. Lewis Jones, of whom the same things may be said. Good or bad, they are not to be judged by the standards of Eisteddfodau or Cymrodorion Societies.

1938

MODESTY

Barbara K. Griffith

Since my arrival here I have learned one thing about the Welsh: that they are too modest. They should advertise themselves more in foreign coutries and let the rest of the world know that Wales is a country with a language, customs and literature of its own, and that it is one of the most beautiful parts of the British Isles. In almost any travel bureau or Steamship Company in the States one will see posters advertising Stratford-on-Avon, the Lake District or Edinburgh. Why shouldn't there be posters of Llandudno, Snowdon and the Swallow Falls? The fact that the Welsh langauge is widely used today in all phases of Welsh life is something that should be made known. A language of its own is one of the outstanding attractions of any country. I am sure that most people in the States, if they bother to think of the Welsh language at all, think of it as a thing of the past, like Cornish, and not one that is spoken widely throughout the country today.

1940

FAMILY FEELING

KENNETH HARRIS

I think that the event which first started me thinking about the Welsh was when I became a newspaper reporter in 1948 and went to live in Sheffield. Up till then I had a quite clear impression in my mind of what Welsh people were like. I looked back on my boyhood days, the memories of which had been refreshed by visits to Wales, and the image was clear. A people of great warmth and neighbourliness above all. A people who lived very close to one another and with a highly developed social sense, of being involved in, and, in often responsible for, the fates of one another. A people of great tenderness and affection. Not placid, not always good tempered; plenty of rows, in village, town or on the national level, but the emotional rows of the kind you find in a family, rather than the calculated and defined quarrels, usually based on a firm sense of incompatibility of personal or political interests which you tend to get in public life in other countries. I never really got over leaving Aberaman, and I know a great many other Welshmen who never recovered that sense of living in an intimate community which every Welsh valley provides, that concern about one another, a bit too nosey at times, you may say, curiosity, inquisitiveness rather than concern.

1956

A RELIGIOUS PEOPLE?

GLYN SIMON
[*Later Archbishop of Wales*]

We are frequently described as a religious people, and I expect that on the whole more people attend public worship on a Sunday in Wales than in England. But that does not necessarily make us a religious people: it would be more true to say that we are a people who like a religious flavour to things; we are certainly not at all clear as to what kind of religion gives the flavour.

It is a long time since we produced a theologian of the first rank, or a devotional writer of eminence, or even, despite many tuneful and charming examples, hymns of that solid content which laid the foundations of Welsh protestantism or enriched the worship of the Welsh Church.

Readers of much modern literature about Wales, or picture-goers, or spectators at a National Eisteddfod, might well suppose, as indeed they do, that if you put a roof over Wales it would cover one large sabbatarian teetotal and Welsh-speaking chapel. But is that really so? Statistics would appear to suggest something very different; our seaside resorts on Sundays are certainly not filled exclusively by the Godless English; and what is the purpose of those very numerous Sunday bus journeys to Herefordshire, Gloucestershire and Shropshire, which are certainly not being made by Englishmen yearning to breathe their native air? And have those particular beliefs an ancestry in Wales of sufficient antiquity to justify the conclusion that they are part and parcel of our national character itself? There has always been a strong ascetic motif in the Welsh character, but it was of a different calibre and rested on a far more secure foundation than what passes for Puritanism in Wales to-day.

1951

MINORITY CULTURE

DANNIE ABSE

Being Jewish in a Welsh community is being as it were a minority within a minority. In London what could I say when they said: "Abse? That's a curious name. Where do you come from? What's your nationality?" Clenching my fists, looking over my shoulder, would I say: 'I'm Welsh'? That would only be half of it. Would I say: 'I'm a Jew'? That wouldn't entirely explain it either. I'd have to say: 'I'm a Welsh Jew or a Jewish Welshman like—well not like Jack Peterson, not like Keir Hardie—but like, well, the Flingelstones and the Cohens and the Isaacs. The Shepherds, the Corns and the Jacobs. The Rubens, the Rivlins, the Rapports and the Roskins. Like Aneurin Levy who lives somewhere between Ystalyfera and Ystrad-mynach, and like Llewellyn ap Goldstein who owns a sweet shop not far from Abercwmboi.'

1955

GRACIOUS LIVING

DR. THOMAS JONES

There is in Ireland an artificial language problem, and I was amused to read a misprint in a recent report of the Irish Council of Education which spoke of Irish as an inflicted language instead of an inflected language.

It is at least doubtful whether in Ireland or in Wales it will be possible to impose bilingualism on the mixed areas. It will almost certainly fail in some where Welsh is not spoken in the home.

Happy is the nation that knows where its real genius lies. In Wales it is not in legislation. It is in its enthusiasm for education, in the widespread diffusion of interest in religion, in the practice of music, poetry and drama, in

10

DANNIE ABSE

Evening Standard Collection
BBC Hulton Picture Library

JOHN ARLOTT

the playing of football. These are exercises in the pursuit of which the world is open to the Welsh to achieve all the excellence they can. Our temptation, living alongside the English, is to exaggerate the importance of the economic motive and to depreciate the artistic aptitudes of our own people, our enthusiasm for a culture at all levels, spread through all classes—adult education in fact.

The Wales which excites my greatest admiration is that of the simple intelligent folk, steeped in our religious tradition, who have mastered the art of life, whether on a farm or in a coalpit or in a shop, who know how to live graciously as good neighbours in quite humble environments. There lies our chief glory. Let us cherish and cultivate these virtues by all the arts of popular education.

1955

TAFFY '66

T. Glynne Davies

Here comes Taffy, fair play to him, still in search of that elusive lump of beef, stumbling over the electronic threshold, bringing with him his coracles, his male voice, his chapel, his bardic gown, his *ch* and his *ll*. Taffy '66 finds himself in an accommodating but strange world which takes for granted a sense of impossible internationalism. Taffy would be the last to deny ideals of international co-operation and goodwill. He would share his last spoonful of *brywes* or *uwd* with anyone. But the internationalism the world believes in—Taffy's world, that is—is far removed from any sense of political idealism.

Internationalism is a social structure in which there is room for one language. That language is an almost monosyllabic form of dropped-h English, as utilitarian as council houses with baths, as immediately communicative as a kiss or a fist in the face. Language, after all

11

these centuries of evolution and experience, has reverted to being no more than a method of instant communication. And this language is used in a society where all middle-aged mothers go, well-bosomed and with hats, to an international bingo hall to be unlucky to lose, where all teenagers have to go, miniskirted or drainpiped, on international scooters, taking their guitars with them on their journey to eternity, and where all daddies sit in raucous unison in grandstands, chanting "Easy! Easy!" while world-cupping internationalists hack each other's legs from under them, before denying with fingers, eyes, and sad horizontal nods that they ever did such a thing.

This, manifestly, is the world we live in: the world in which Taffy finds himself protesting from his plantation of council houses, but the world that even his children are in danger of accepting.

Give up, Taffy. It's a dead language. Petrol pump is pwmp petrol, atomic bomb is bom atomig, a tin of salmon is tun o samwn. And what is the Welsh word for "bingo"? Ha ha.

It was so much easier for Taffy in the old days, when culture was a rich antidote to poverty and boredom, when people were in each other's screenless, discless company for so many sad, grey hours on end that language had to be more than a way of saying, "Open a tin of beans, love!"

Taffy '66 will tell you with bursting pride that his grandfather was no mere robot with a beard. He may even bore you with his tales of quarrymen meeting on quarry premises to pray and discuss theology and literature, of housewives in sack aprons discussing on their doorsteps not the price of over-ripe tomatoes and the mathematical injustices of bingo, but whether Nebuchadnezzar and Lazarus, had they coincided in the accident of time, would have been socially on speaking terms. I am certain that these nostalgic reminiscences are a little overloaded with enthusiasm, that they have about them something of

12

the grace of Greek legend. Only the gods are transferred into peasant women in shawls and gold-rimmed oval-lensed spectacles, anchored to buttermilk kitchens where the windows have geraniums and the chairs anti-macassars.

The truth is that Taffy's grandparents were in love with language and the expression of moods. They built up a peasant culture unequalled in Western existence. We have the proof today in the remarkable inheritance of poetic volumes and in the tradition that persists in some rural cases. We had the proof too in those politicians who surfaced above the level of the oak pulpit. That is why Taffy '66 still expands as he speaks of the *werin*, not knowing that it died with the geraniums.

The *gwerin*—the mass of ordinary people, all enlightened and thirsty for culture and learning was a substantial fact. It was also peasantry, essentially rural. With the second generation of urban existence it was bound to diminish in importance and die, because an industrial, urban proletariat will always swallow and strangle any *gwerin* that the hinterland spews up. The world of '66 belongs to the town and to economics and industry. Our form of democracy dictates that it must be so. Rural areas are fields of agricultural production primarily; beyond that they become exciting playgrounds that can be developed with lakes, boats, concrete paths and ice-cream kiosks for the smoked out proletariat of the industrial areas.

1966

13

PUZZLED OF BRYNSIENCYN

Ian Skidmore

What I do not understand is how the National Eisteddfod, which is racial intolerance set to music, can possibly object to a member of its ruling body taking a choir to South Africa; the country which invented the dictum of loathe thy fellow men.

And I admit to being puzzled to know why the International Eisteddfod, which is built on a principle of international goodwill and has steadily ignored prejudice over an area which has stretched from Russia to Swaziland, should have bowed to the fashionable boycott of singers from South Africa.

Rational men would have taken a view that the only suitable subject for boycotting is the boycott; a device of the junior common room and like that ludicrous community quite divorced from real life. Singers, indeed creative people of any kind, are happily so obsessed by their own subject that they have little time for unimportant areas like politics. And practically the only favourable thing one can say about sportsmen is that they aren't interested in politics either. The politically hyperactive are so endowed to console them for having little else to offer the world at large.

But of course there is nothing even remotely rational about the Eisteddfod. The word means sitting down place and seems a curiously inept description of a festival where everyone walks in an endless Impi, circling the pavilion like musical bees; a poetry festival in which for a week not a single line of the competitors' poetry is heard —only adjudications.

If you want to judge the winning poem for yourself, you have to buy a book to read it.

It is as though the Derby were to be run in the Stewards' Enclosure, watched only by the Duke of Norfolk and his colleagues; and wagers settled on their view of who should win it. The National Eisteddfod is—delightful prospect—a test match where the cricketers are hidden from view and only the voice of the commentator is heard in the land. And if the Eisteddfod itself is a puzzle to the rational mind, the Gorsedd of the Bards of Great Britain is the ultimate production in the summer season of the Theatre of the Absurd.

Firstly the title of this assembly of Welsh-speaking Bedouins is a misnomer, unless you perceive Great Britain as being that narrow strip of land between Offa's Dyke and the Irish Sea. Barnsley Bards or Ovates from Arundel are at a premium. And I live in the pious hope that some day someone will be able to explain why the stones round which they troop like troubled Tauregs represent the twelve tribes of Israel and the one in the centre of the Ark of the Covenant.

I know that the Eisteddfod is the joint creation of those epic fantasists Iolo Morganwg and Cynan, who introduced the pageantry and was to our national festival what Flo Zeigfield was to those other musical follies on Broadway. What *can* one say about a cry for peace from a man who is holding a giant sword; indeed about the whole ceremony which fuses the frolics of the Woodland Folk scattering petals with the mumbo-jumbo of Freemasonry; an evocation so powerful that one waits with bated breath for the Archdruid to roll up his trouser leg and the Crowned Bard to frankly expose his bust.

I know that practically the only growth industry in Wales has been the invention of its own history; forged— in every sense of the word—in the fires of its own powerful fancy. But one would have liked to have peered further into the mists of history than the 18th century—and in a different direction than Primrose Hill on the outskirts of London for the origins of our national festival.

It must be said that even so it is earlier than most English ceremonial; and indeed it wasn't until some time later that Sir Walter Scott invented the Scottish Highlands for the sake of the German who ruled England.

1986

WAITING FOR DAI

HENRY HIGGINS

I believe that the love of idealism and quietude, characteristic of the Welsh, could contribute to the improvement of the more forceful disposition of the English. Similarly, the tendency to irresolution and delay, which is characteristic of my Welsh neighbours, would benefit from an infusion of the qualities of persistence and self-assertiveness of the English people. The fusion of differing national qualities can be mutually advantageous to both peoples. History tells us that mixed races are most virile and progressive, whereas self-contained static nations, like elderly persons, are inclined to live much in the past. Consequently, matters that should be taken in hand at once are commonly postponed in the hope that someone will do what is needed, or that something will happen to cancel the necessity for further action.

This spirit of continuous deferment of responsibility has developed an ingenuity in the construction of excuses. These are usually referred to as "explanations" which means that the work that should be done and which often is generously suggested is relegated to an indefinite future. In the smaller communities this spirit is too frequently in evidence in the neglect even of local benefits provided by incomers or secured by public subscriptions. Musical instruments, fire extinguishing appliances are bundled away in empty rooms, churchyards wrested from the original owners under the Cemeteries Act, are all allowed to get into a deplorable condition; even playing fields are permitted to become weed plantations, and paths have become almost unusable because of the lack of a proper sense of responsibility.

I also see in this Iberic heritage an explanation of the numerous futile public meetings that are held and which seldom serve any better purpose than to reveal a general lack of unanimity even in purely local matters. After all, the faults I have mentioned are to the disadvantage of the people themselves rather than to others. It may be that I have looked in the wrong direction for the source of these weaknesses. It might be claimed as being traceable to the feudal system in which the labouring classes were encouraged to look to the overlords for relief whenever trouble occurred. But all that could be claimed for such an assumption is as applicable to most of the county districts of England. I prefer to regard the influence of that system as having encouraged rather than originated this lack of a sense of responsibility. To whatever cause the fault may be traceable it is a real and grievous one that can only be mastered by an increased infusion of a more progressive spirit.

1937

SEEING CLEARLY

CLOUGH WILLIAMS-ELLIS

We Welsh are generally a bit lop-sided in our culture—we have, perhaps, like most Celts, attended so much to literature, music, drama and oratory that the *visual* arts have been crowded out so that where there might be another whole enjoyable slice of life there is just a blank. Maybe we are still suffering from the old Puritan prejudice that counted delight of the eye as a snare of impiety and worldliness—so we are still mistrustful of it.

Anyway we do seem mostly pretty blind and indifferent to visual beauty, do little to create it, and are far slacker in the care of our precious heritage of natural beauty than good patriots ought to be. Dull eyes indeed are not merely a personal handicap. They are a danger to Wales itself, for they accept without dismay or protest all sorts of indignities, the cruel and permanent disfiguring of our land by unworthy buildings, needlessly ugly exploitations and developments of all kinds, industrial and other—gross discourtesies in town and country that we should indignantly resent if we were, visually, more sensitive and alert. Often it's a matter of undoing what was ill done in the recent even darker past—by our own fathers or grandfathers—for we do now at least see better than they did.

1953

HUMILITY AND THE COUNCILLOR

ALEX GORDON

As I see it the breadth of outlook of many of our councillors leaves a lot to be desired. The dominance of the professional committee man discourages many responsible citizens from putting themselves forward for election, and there is a progressive lowering in standards. There is a tendency for local authorities to become concerned too much with detail and to fail to give the correct consideration to matters of importance.

There is insufficient awareness in cultural matters, coupled with a lack of humility (a quality which is generally absent in small minded people and highly developed in the truly great). This results in a tendency to interfere in matters about which they know little, and disinclination to seek advice.

It is surely ridiculous for elected representatives to have an authority in aesthetic matters when they have never really studied the subject. I know that the officials of some authorities are attempting to educate their members by lectures and showings of coloured slides, but I would like to see every councillor subjected to an examination in visual awareness, breadth of outlook and knowledge of what is going on elsewhere in the world before he is permitted to take a decision affecting any form of development. You will notice that I do not say express an opinion (every person is free to do this) but a decision which affects the work of others is a very serious thing indeed.

In my view the decline in breadth of outlook in the council chamber has gone too far for us to expect much change of heart by the injection of new blood and as I see it the only hope for improvement, in so far as planning and visual matters are concerned is to limit the authority and powers of the local councils. I make a strong plea for stricter physical control of development (where you may build what) on a regional basis, but in order to improve aesthetic standards, in order to discourage restrictive parochialism, less authority for interference by untrained lay committees.

Let those who consider these views too harsh and unfair and perhaps even unbalanced look around and ask themselves what benefits the present controls have brought. Could our post war urban sprawl have been worse? Is our countryside really being preserved as well as it might? Are the problems of the motor car being fully appreciated, let alone solved, and is any thought being given now to the problems which our present economic success and expansion will bring?

1961

DICTATORSHIP BY COMMITTEE

Dr. Thomas Jones

Religion, education, and machinery are great levellers. Religion proclaims the eternal worth of the common man; education destroys distinctions based on birth, rank and wealth; the cultured man moves easily in any society, rich, middling, or poor; and when you walk in a Cardiff park or on the seafront at Llandudno you can hardly tell to-day the class to which persons belong from their clothes. Machinery has brought this about. This is a victory of quantity. Can we make it a victory of quality?

For some important purposes it is right to treat men as equal. But we know that if it be true that men are very like one another, the little difference may be all-important. Where the difference is great you get the extraordinary person. And these extraordinary persons are those who are the instruments of the big changes in human progress. The charge against democracy is that while it elevates the common man it abuses and ill-treats the exceptional man. It discounts eminence and excellence. I said at the Neath Eisteddfod that in a hundred years, perhaps I ought to have said in a thousand, Wales had produced but two men of world-wide significance, Robert Owen and Lloyd George. It is impossible to measure the value of the contribution which genius makes to civilization. Sir James Jeans, speaking as President of the British Association at Aberdeen a few weeks ago, said that it had been estimated that the economic value of one scientist alone, Edison, had been put at £3,000,000,000. It is certain that men like Faraday and Clerk Maxwell have created social values equal to the labour of millions of ordinary men. But there is no prescription for the production of genius.

Mr. Lloyd George has been compared to a force of nature. Such forces cannot be produced to order. But short of producing men of such exceptional power, can more be done for the man who is above the average? We are extending equality of opportunity to lower levels of the population. Can we give special, unequal opportunity in Wales to the exceptional, take greater care of the unusual person who promises to grow well above the ordinary and commonplace? Are we doing our utmost to cherish excellence and distinction wherever we find it? How should it be done? It is easier to point out ways in which we are discouraging distinction in our midst and driving it across the border. This is putting in another way the question: How are we to cure democracy of one of its chief defects: its preference for mediocrity?

Take the question of appointments. No week passes in which public men do not receive letters asking them to support for public posts persons whom they have never seen, sometimes have never heard of, and of those qualifications they have no first-hand knowledge whatsoever. It has become almost impossible to place any reliance on testimonials even though written by Ministers of the Gospel. The desire to be kind drives out the desire to be honest. Instead of producing two great men in a century we are, according to these testimonials, producing two every week.

You have a similar result when tests are applied in making appointments which have nothing to do with the qualities required for the post. For example, you appoint a schoolmaster because he is a Methodist, or a Freemason, or a Socialist, not because he is a good schoolmaster. This is an old and widespread abuse and it has the effect of discouraging the best candidates. Bad money drives out good. So much has this evil habit developed that it is notorious that while lip service has to be paid to the forms of democracy by advertising posts, those who are determined to get the best men devise other means of discovering them.

The essence of the abuse is that you introduce a test which restricts the field of choice—it may be to a denomination or to a political party. Where a political party is overwhelmingly strong you have in effect a new form of dictatorship—the dictatorship of committees who speak with one voice and who suppress all attempts at real freedom of choice. In recent years the restriction has been applied to a locality—this is parochialism reduced to absurdity. A boy or girl is drawn from, let us say, an area in Blankshire, goes through a training college, and because he comes from Blankshire and has been supported by the county, he expects to have a job in the county and feels a grievance if he doesn't get it. Merthyr posts for Merthyr boys, Rhymney posts for Rhymney girls, and so forth. This is to discourage free trade in brains and the results are thoroughly bad.

Less than a hundred years ago the possession of a university degree lifted a man high above his fellows. Didn't Joseph Thomas, Carno, express his astonishment when he discovered that Dr. Lewis Edwards slept (or snored) like an ordinary mortal? To-day degrees are as common as blackberries in autumn. Students come up for graduation not one by one but in battalions on graduation day. Every year sees seven hundred new graduates in Wales. But the notion that a pass degree means something very difficult of attainment is still widespread. When it is obtained the parents feel society ought to reward their son with a black-coated and soft-handed job. They are bitterly disappointed when that does not happen. In other words the public does not sufficiently realize that as the net is spread and the number of graduates multiplies the quality tends to fall. A recent enquiry conducted by the Carnegie Foundation in the United States into the intelligence of undergraduates has led to this conclusion: "The American college degree means almost nothing as a standard of educational development." A similar enquiry in Wales would certainly not yield a more favourable result.

Graduates from Wales who come to London to seek their fortunes are more likely to break down in the personal interview when qualities other than the possession of knowledge are tested. Knowledge without personality is at a discount in the open market. Graduates are legion, personalities are rare.

We have four university colleges; they cater mainly for the ordinary student. The good result of having four colleges in Wales is that they are within easy reach of the population and degrees can be obtained at a cheap rate. The bad result is that all four have to cover very much of the same ground. The provision of honours work has to be triplicated or quadrupled. Two highly equipped colleges might in some respects have been better than four. But the four are there. Is it impossible for the new Principal of Aberystwyth to frame his policy in such a way as to raise the standards at Aberystwyth? Can we have one uncommon college where the whole emphasis is on the honours man? At present the University finances are so ordered that grants move upwards with the number of students. That again is a premium on quantity instead of quality. Some of us would welcome a decline in the number of students at Aberystwyth provided the proportion of uncommon students increased.

The most interesting educational experiment in the United States at the moment is that of Dr. Flexner at Princeton. He has been given a vast endowment in order to produce an Institute of Advanced Study. It is a protest against the debasement of universities. At Princeton there will be no undergraduates and no examinations, and the list of professors is headed by Einstein. It is a tremendous bid not for numbers but for distinction, for the exceptional student and the exceptional professor. No millionaire has yet endowed Principal Ifor Evans. But short of that, can he take Aberystwyth some distance along the Princeton path? We might then have a few more uncommon Welshmen.

1934

23

CARWYN

ALUN RICHARDS

To taxi drivers, groundsmen, the high and mighty in the President's box or the thousands on the terraces in rugby grounds all over the world, he was simply Carwyn—just that. Even the funeral notice announced: "Carwyn funeral Monday."

There were golden qualities about him both private and public. He was the most approachable of men, uniquely devoid of consciousness of rank or title, without side or pretence, a rare South Walian trait that made him at once loved and at the same time especially vulnerable to those who wanted not so much to listen to him as to forcibly express their own opinions. These he avoided when he decently could and when he walked into a room a way cleared, not because of a sense of awe for he was the mildest of celebrities but because those who knew him, however slightly, immediately warmed to him.

Many famous Welshmen are rightly known for rhetoric, the forensic command of language that ignites those bonded in common cause, but he would have none of this, never raised his voice and listened far more than he spoke.

If there was any one phrase to describe him in company it was his persistent unobtrusiveness. He never pushed and yet at times he was everywhere, always with this charisma that left you with the feeling of uplift which was the hallmark of the most princely of his gifts—friendship. You never saw him without the feeling that he was glad to see you, that no matter how unexpected the encounter he had arrived especially to lighten your day. When he smiled it was with his whole face, often nodding intently as if the smile was not enough, hurrying forward, a cigarette never far away, often a glass in hand for he was the most convivial of men. This was the physical presence, the smile and gaze so genuine that you learnt to ignore the manifestations of the painful and incurable skin disease which haunted him day and night, so much so that he decided to ignore it and became unembarrassed himself—the only cure he knew.

All this was why we all felt his passing so deeply, almost all his friends in precisely the same way, for what we had lost was the instigator and agent of a better reflection of ourselves—this another of the Carwyn gifts as catalyst. Quite simply, he brought the best out in people. This was his forte, especially with young people, for they have a more direct way of knowing who is genuinely interested in them and who is not. For so many of them he was a man who always found the time—trains, buses, flight could wait. What was more important than the person in front of you?

So on vegetable garden cricket patches, street corners and odd playgrounds, the dustbin cricketer who would bowl legbreaks by the hour to ten year olds was another man with another ambience—to say nothing of rugby's Father Christmas who distributed international tickets, ties, trinkets, even track suits like sweets. Any other man would have had a lot of explaining to do but not Carwyn —certainly not Carwyn.

He was also, of course, an enigma, more of a wayward artist than any of the job descriptions that went with his career as a teacher or broadcaster. He was a miner's son who once took up the cudgels against the Coal Board on behalf of his silicotic father, a rugby coach who went at it like an obsessed philosopher, a bon viveur for whom asparagus was the only really edible vegetable, a principal feeder of persons who sat next to him at dinners and functions across the world. He had a special fly half's sleight-of-hand for wrapping and passing half a steak under the tablecloth and, above all, he was a champion and unpredictable daytime sleeper.

He was also a marathon smoker of repute and, when not

looked after by his sister Gwen, he gathered ash, unwashed glasses and debris around him like a walking Vesuvius.

Abroad in Italy, where I got to know him best, you could not get into his room because he filed the jackets of suits, sports coats, dressing gowns on the edge of the door, while the trousers blossomed like plants in the window. There were always letters opened and unopened, rugby programmes and the currencies of all the rugby-playing countries in the world decorating the floor together with old cheques, usually uncashed, as well as the four or five books he was reading simultaneously. He cared not a jot for things. Possessions were meaningless and a nuisance. When it suited him he left suitcases where they fell—dotted about the world.

And yet, for all this, he was a deeply serious man and in many ways his rugby career was a relaxation that became a profession because he had failed as a politician who wanted to change the way we in Wales live now. He never wavered in his nationalism and he was a critic, too, in private as well as in public. I can hear his voice now. "This is turning into a weepie, Richards." Well, not yet, not quite.

He was also, of course, a scream. The only man I ever knew who fell asleep on the pillion seat of a motor cycle. I knew because I was driving. As I leaned one way he sagged the other, a hazardous practice which was repeated several times. This habit of falling asleep he indulged in everywhere. He slept at the opera, at functions, at the table in restaurants between courses. And although I thought it a recent habit, and put it down to the fact that he had not had an unbroken night's sleep in years because of his cruel skin infection, I was told it was not so. As a young lecturer he once fell asleep in a tutorial in the presence of a student who waited for an hour to ask him a final question. That was Carwyn—always worth waiting for.

SIR GERAINT EVANS

Evening Standard Collection
BBC Hulton Picture Library

GWYN THOMAS

Evening Standard Collection
BBC Hulton Picture Library

Now he is gone. On reflection it is not totally unexpected. He was not very interested in looking after himself.

"I've had a good life," he told me by chance a few weeks ago. "I have no regrets."

There was very little he didn't know about himself and, I'm sure, how much we cared for him. A vulnerable man of such gentleness of spirit, kindness and sensitivity could want no more.

1983

ALUN LEWIS

GWYN JONES

By his death the English-speaking world has lost a poet of real achievement and great promise; Wales has lost one of his finest sons; and all who knew him have lost some enrichment of their personalities.

He breathed literature; it was the air in his lungs, the blood in his veins; and yet we know he was a man of action too. This is perhaps the true measure of our loss in him: here was a writer who saw and felt as only poets can, and who, despite his youth, had lived through cycles of experience. Each year he grew increasing master of his crafts. How delicate and strong a lyric like this: the title poem of *Raiders' Dawn*:

> Softly the civilised
> Centuries fall,
> Paper on paper,
> Peter on Paul.
>
> And lovers waking
> From the night—
> Eternity's masters,
> Slaves of Time—

Recognise only
The drifting white
Fall of small faces
In pits of lime.

Blue necklace left
On a charred chair
Tells that Beauty
Was startled there.

He had the gift, the divine gift of poetry; he was working free from the merely literary influences that can be seen in his earliest writing; and the war years had matured him as he might not have matured in ten years of peace. His term of service in India had clearly produced a new Alun Lewis. I quote from the last letter I had from him: "I've grown older and humbler out here, and expect less of life than I did once." He was always open to the impulse of pity—for the weak, the exploited, the dumb and suffering millions of all colours and creeds whose unheeded lives and deaths are but compost about the roots of history. You will find this love and pity—and there is nothing for which we should more honour any man—in many of the published poems, in stories like *Private Jones* and *They Came*—that study in violence and horror which yet ends on so glorious a note of love and reconciliation —the young Welsh soldier who, after war has plunged him into an unimaginable hell, can yet cry out in faith: "My life belongs to the world. I will do what I can."

1944

DAVID JONES

Harman Grisewood

In the BBC Wales radio lecture for 1965, Harman Grise-
wood examined the work and philosophy of David Jones,
the writer and artist.

It is not mere accident that the artist whose work we are
discussing is a poet who was once a soldier. Nor is it mere
accident, that his theme is partly historical and is partly
about the nature of man. For, if our present predicament
involves a re-appraisal of history, that effort must lead
to some consideration of our beliefs and purpose, and so to
some consideration of what is natural to men who hold
those beliefs and who are prepared to act upon them.

Most would agree that our age is typified by technology,
yet few feel anything but misgiving at a prospect of
domination by technological man. Pride in our achievements is matched by fear that they may destroy us. This
fear is not confined to the effects of nuclear weapons. We
fear—many of us—an enslavement to the machine and a
corresponding mechanisation of our humanity. We are
led to wonder what it is that can be relied on to disting-
uish our own human nature from our already mechanised
environment. The terms which have upheld the distinction
so far are less and less available to the community as
a whole. They are theological, or humanistic in the
Renaissance sense, or they are merely subjective and
sentimental.

Mr. David Jones opens up a rather different approach.
In the *Anathemata* he invites us to contemplate man as a
maker of things. The things which a man makes testify
and assert the humanity of the maker as distinct from the
works of animals or the other operations of nature.

The evidence for the distinction, Mr. Jones explains, is
a quality which he terms the gratuitous. The gratuitous is
a quality given voluntarily for no recompense. It is a

quality that is different from the utilitarian. It is an intransitive quality, yet it has significance for the maker and for the beholder. It is a sign. In the development of this thesis, Mr. Jones shows that man-the-maker is by his essential humanity a maker of signs, and that man the sign maker is man the artist.

There would be nothing very new or surprising in seeking a distinction between man and animal in the endowments of the artist. Aesthetic pleasure and aesthetic creation have been exalted time and again as a contrast to what some call our animal natures. But what was usually meant by that distinction is the exaltation of a spiritual quality in contrast to a carnal or terrestrial one. We are all familiar with the aesthetic outlook in which the priest is replaced by the artist, art works are substituted for the evidence of religion and an aesthetic afflatus is made to do the work of religious exercise. It was nothing more than the old contrast of mind and matter.

Now, Mr. Jones will have none of this. Art and the practices of art are for him as carnal and terrestrial as a camp of soldiers. The purpose of art is not a state of mind but a thing, as tangible and visible as a piece of cake or a pair of stockings. Indeed, Mr. Jones insists that the lady in the kitchen or with her needle and thread uses the faculties of the artist, and in what she is doing she has more in common with Michelangelo or Virgil than with the patient beaver constructing his dam of twigs across the stream. The result, Mr. Jones declares, is decisive in its evidence of humanity. In an important essay to be found in a collection of his occasion pieces Mr. Jones illustrates what he is saying by writing of a cook icing a cake with an S for Susan's birthday. He imagines the cook saying, "This is for Susan's birthday. Don't you think it a work of art?" He continues: "You may or may not agree with the cook's notion of beauty but you would not be able to deny the 'art'. For learning aside, the art of cooking and the supererogatory art of icing, in so far as the cake is made for Susan's birthday, it is 'made over' in some sense." He goes on "All the conditions determining what is art from what is not, are fulfilled. There is making, there is added marking, there is explicit sign, there is a showing forth, a re-presenting, a re-calling, a gratuitousness and there is a full intention to make this making thus."

1965

CARADOC EVANS

GEORGE BULLOCK

My first remembrance of Caradoc Evans is of a tall, bony-looking man with grey upstanding hair who, after he had been in the room only a short time, began attacking me for not liking the Welsh. His wife was speaking to me about one of his books when he sharply interrupted her with: "He doesn't like my books. He's only interested in highbrows."

Now the disconcerting thing for me was that this judgment was correct. In those days I couldn't stand Caradoc Evans's stories about the Welsh. Like a lot of English people I disliked books written in any sort of dialect, and the biting satire of *My People* was lost to me entirely. But of course I made polite protestation, only to find myself a few minutes later in another embroilment. Fleet Street was mentioned and I made a slighting reference to journalism. Caradoc immediately pounced on me and shouted like an Old Testament prophet with a Welsh accent: "What's the matter with journalism? It's a grand profession! All the best writers are journalists."

I can't remember my reply to this sweeping pronounce-ment, but I know it wasn't long before I realised that the man who talked so wildly liked argument for its own sake, and often made exaggerated statements to be provoking. For about two hours we disagreed with each

31

other and, in spite of the obvious antagonism between us, enjoyed ourselves a great deal. I remember very well the exhilarated feelings with which I left at the end of the afternoon. Every part of my mind felt exercised, and although after that first meeting I may not have been able to say with any sincerity that I liked Caradoc Evans, I certainly respected him.

In the next few months I saw quite a lot of him and his wife. I stayed weekends with them, and had a chance of getting to know Caradoc better. A rather wary attitude towards each other prevented us being real friends, yet I don't think he was ever not pleased to see me and I, for my part, thoroughly enjoyed being with him. He was an exciting, stimulating person even when he chose to be what we call "difficult." There was a perverse side to his make-up which delighted in sending a conversation awry. On the other hand he was always ready to hand out praise because, I think, he liked to see people pleased with themselves and with him. In his passionate self, and the demoniac force with which he attacked things or people who annoyed him, he reminded me of D. H. Lawrence. He seemed at times to inhabit a different universe from that of most men—an intenser world where everything glowed and burned more fiercely. And like Lawrence he had the power of making simple things appear wonderful. In his company one was never dull; exasperated perhaps sometimes when he persisted in hammering a point longer than was necessary; but bored—never. His zest for life was violent and his high spirits infectious; but darker moods sometimes took possession of him and then he could be mocking and savage.

He had the idea at first that I was a young highbrow, a member of a select coterie, who turned up his nose at anything ordinary. Because of this he was inclined to treat me derisively. He spoke mockingly of the writers I praised, and himself professed admiration for several women novelists whose work is not usually considered important. "At least you get real emotion in their books," he used to say, although at the time I was writing a book criticising one of them, and he'd given me many helpful suggestions.

I remember Sunday Mornings when he threw the *Observer* at me across the table saying: "Here you are—here's your paper." Then taking the *News of the World* with rather a show, he added: "This is the best of the lot. You get real life in here—not a lot of highbrow stuff."

1948

GWYN THOMAS

Gwyn Jones

He was the most remarkable talker in certain ways that I've ever heard. I don't know where this perpetual fountain or lava flow of phrase, wisdom, nonsense came from. Sometimes a deliberately Socratic zanydom poured out of him which was still edged with every kind of overtone and undertone of wisdom, pity, a touch of malevolence occasionally, wilfulness; an entirely remarkable man.

Let's put it this way, the rest of us are very happy if we coin a good phrase from time to time. These poured out of Gwyn, perhaps too frequently. I think in the course of an hour he would use as many remarkable phrases as most people use in a year, ten years, or an entire lifetime. You know they say that man is a dancing animal, man is a singing animal and things of this kind. Gwyn was a talking animal. His books in a sense are an extension of his talking. His talk was not an extension of his books, his books were an extension of his talk. It seemed to me this was a kind of writing I had never read before. Insofar as it reminded me of other writers there was this feeling of abundance that came out of it. When you read Mark Twain, for example, another humorist who is a very serious man in much of his writing, you have this same feeling.

There's a great deal of it there and it's not going to dry up and you felt that about Gwyn. You also felt this strange mixture of deliberate folly in the sense that it was cultivated comicality in expression with much wisdom and deep feeling. I'd never read anything like it.

1981

AN ARTIST FATHER

Wynford Vaughan-Thomas

When I start remembering my father, a clear picture comes at once to my mind. I see myself back again with him in his study in our house in Swansea. There is the fire burning briskly in the grate. The light flickers on the rows of books, the manuscripts half-written on the desk. And I am sitting with father at the piano, trying to play the easy part in one of Mozart's symphonies, arranged as a piano duet.

I must have been about eleven at the time, and father was just starting to write his *cywyddau*—those settings of poems by Dafydd ap Gwilym, William Llŷn and the others, which I always think are amongst the loveliest of all his music. He'd start to work on them during the evening, and continue late into the night. He'd been smoking his inevitabvle cigarette—for father was a chain-smoker once he started to compose. He'd be perpetually on the move between the piano and the writing desk, altering a phrase, trying a more effective combination of chords. And we listening, as we did our homework in the next room would hear the new song taking shape through the evening—to the ruin of our homework, I can tell you!

But just before we went to bed, mother would make up a tray of tea and Welsh cakes and let me carry it into the study. This was my great moment. Father would take a break, and I'd sit at the piano with him to try my hand at Mozart before being packed off upstairs. I say try my hand because father was a fine pianist, and my part was confined to putting in a few uncertain notes in the bass.

But under father's hands, a clear stream of lucid music would flow through the room, and I would be seized with illusions of grandeur. I imagined that I was really playing those symphonies; and once, when we ended a particularly triumphant finale, I remember turning to father and saying: "Do you think I could ever write like that?" Father took my hands and smiled very gently as he said: "No, I don't think you should ever be an artist. It would hurt you too much."

I have often remembered those words of his. When he spoke them, he must have realised that he would never be a success in the material sense of the word. Maybe he'd begun to see that Wales would never give him that official post with a steady income, however small, which he needed to get leisure for his true work—his composing. He'd been hurt all right. But at the time I thought he was joking.

I didn't believe him for one moment. I went upstairs to bed and until I fell asleep I could hear him at work again, playing and replaying (and singing in his finely controlled light baritone voice) *Y Nos*—The Night. And I thought how wrong father was, and how lucky I was to have an artist for a father. It made me somehow different—far superior—to the other boys at school, whose fathers simply kept shops or sat in offices all day, and who couldn't even start to play the piano. I didn't know any better at eleven!

1949

35

A SINGER'S TRAGEDY

Gwen Ffrangcon-Davies

In 1949, the actress Gwen Ffrangcon-Davies recalled her father, David Ffrangcon-Davies, a celebrated baritone whose career was cut short by illness and who died in 1918.

How much I regret that my father's career was in the days before recording. What a joy it would have been to listen to his glorious voice now. I was only a child when his career ended so tragically, and yet I can hear it now after all these years. What a thrilling timbre it had when he sang in Gerontius: "Go forth upon thy journey Christian Soul." I have never heard just that quality of conviction and sincerity since. It was I suppose because he believed and felt so deeply what he sang.

Those early performances of Gerontius with father and Gervase Elwes were more than just performances—they were almost a religious observance—something one will never forget. It was this quality of dedication that made father's singing so memorable. His work was his life, and everything else, even human relationships, had to take second place. He had two profound interests—his music and his study of philosophy and metaphysics. He was a deeply thoughtful and religious man—in his later years his pre-occupation with metaphysics became an abnormal one—indeed it was a symptom of the mental disturbance that cut short his career at the height of his power.

It is in a way difficult for me to talk about my father, because in a sense we always remained strangers. As little children, except for one summer in Berlin, we saw little of him. We were in the nursery and he was often away. Later, when we might have been able to be companions for him, he became even more pre-occupied with his career, and I personally was too diffident and timid ever to feel at ease with him.

Looking back I can remember being amazed when sometimes the child of one of my father's friends would visit us and treat him with an easy familiarity that I could never achieve. Though I was barely fifteen when his illness took him away from us, I could sense his greatness as an artist without being able to get near him as a man.

The last ten years of his life were terribly sad, for he suffered from acute melancholia, and it used to wring my heart to see him and not be able to help him. He was so broken, so pitiful and gentle. He did get very much better and indeed was expecting to start singing again—for his voice was as beautiful as ever after the long rest—but it was not to be, and he died very suddenly one morning from heart failure. I think perhaps the Gods were kind, for he died happy in the prospect of starting work again, and the reality might have been too much for him.

There was certainly a magic and a magnetism about him. He was a great artist and had all his life been encouraged to believe that he was a law unto himself. If he could have perhaps taken life and himself a little less seriously he would have been a happier person—but he was an exceptional man—not to be measured by ordinary standards. He gave something great to the world and paid a great price in giving it.

1949

AN EISTEDDFOD CONFRONTATION

SIR GERAINT EVANS

I remember a big eisteddfod in the Workman's Hall one year. My father's choir, the Handel Glee Party, were running the competition and it went on throughout the day.

In the evening they had the Champion Solo competition, where the tenor and the contralto and the soprano and the bass would compete against each other and be given the medal for the winner—the Champion of that day. I was only a small boy, and because I was the son of the conductor I had to present the medal to the winner.

The person the audience thought should have had the prize—indeed, *she* thought she should have had the prize, wasn't given it. It was given to the contralto, and while I was beginning to place the medal on this lovely ribbon around he neck, the soprano came barging in.

She was like an Italian; she was big, she had black black hair with a bun at the back, and a fantastic voice, there's no question about it. But the adjudicators were judging her on musicality, on interpretation.

As I was presenting the medal to the contralto, this soprano came in and she pushed me on one side, medal as well, and she pointed to the gallery where the adjudicators were and said: "If I'd a gun I'd shoot the bloody lot of you," and walked off.

I was terrified. *Cythrel Canu*—the Devil in Song.

1984

INFLUENCES

WYNFORD VAUGHAN-THOMAS

Looking back on it when I was a young man, rather as a young boy really, there was a wonderful folk singer in Gower called Phil Tanner and he used to sing these wonderful old folk songs sitting outside the bar of the Kings Head in Llangennech on a warm summer evening. He taught me that there was zest in life and that there was gusto and thrill in life.

Then, I think in the War, the chap who took me in his aircraft over Berlin was a formative influence on me in a curious way because he taught me what courage was. Ken Letford, the captain, was so cool. He'd been thirty-three times to Berlin already and was going to go fifty-two times.

He controlled that aircraft, his voice still for all the excitement, and there we were moving—well—sort of festering, a hellish mess really, and that man had inside him reserves of courage that kept us all going and I admired that.

Then of the great men one's met I think the one who impressed me most was Nehru. There was a leader of men. A very handsome man too, a man of wit, a man who could see through the human values. I'll never forget on the day before the handover of power, Mountbatten gave a tremendous reception.

I was fortunate enough to walk for a brief moment with Nehru and I said: "Sir," rather boldly. "Tomorrow you'll be the man of power. What do you hope for your country?"

He gave me a wicked look and that marvellous smile he had and he said: "Sometimes when I think of my problems ahead I wish that there would fall from the pitiless blue Indian sky of my unhappy country a remorseless shower of contraceptives."

I think we've got to be optimists. I mean people are now wringing their hands, they assume that the nuclear holocaust is going to take place. Now this may be—I may be proved wrong at this very moment but I feel that the very fact that these nuclear weapons exist—rather like gas in the last war—people are hesitating to use them and it's keeping a peace of sorts. Somehow I think that there will come a deal between the two blocks that now possess the world, the two ideologies. I feel that there will be—for want of a better word—I don't want to use the word spiritual because I'm not a religious man, but I think there will be a turn around, that people will need some better ideals than they've got at the moment.

I am a stupidly old-fashioned optimist, old enough to be an optimist perhaps. I think I'd like to see the world another twenty years on. I'll never forget my grandfather, who was an old rebel who led the Rebecca Riots, the riots that used to destroy tollgates back in 1839 in Wales.

The old rebel then, of course, had to reform and on his death bed the minister came to him and said: "Mr. Lewis, you're going to see your Maker face to face."

My grandfather said: "Can you assure me of that?"

The minister said: "Mr. Lewis, if ever a man is going to see his Maker face to face, you are that man."

My grandfather's last words were: "Well, in that case there are one or two pertinent questions I'm going to put to Him."

1983

DEATH OF A MINER

FLORENCE HUMPHREYS

I was holding a hand between both mine, soaping it with warm fragrant soapsuds, then carefully drying it with a clean towel. It was a hand still hard and calloused to the touch, but now thin with the silver transparency of a birch tree in winter. It was my father's hand. He lay dying and he knew it. His body was just tired out: but for all that he was deeply aware, as though the quintessence of life lay in these last sips. I put one hand on the eiderdown and began washing the other. We were both watching this procedure.

"Do you remember lifting us on to the Rocking Stone on the common, and giving us rides on it, Dad?" I asked.

When we were children he used to take us on to the common which overlooks the town. Here, there are two huge stones, one flat and circular, supporting the other, also circular but rounded at the base. There was a time many, many years ago, when even the wind would set it rocking to and fro, so delicately balanced was it. But when we were children dirt had clogged the rocking stone so that it took a man of considerable strength to set it in motion. These frail hands that I was washing had lifted us up, a group of laughing children, and had rocked the massive thing like a rollicking wooden horse in a nursery. How he had loved doing it!

The firm lips broke into a smile.

"Well, Dad, the strongest man alive couldn't budge it now. It's clogged up fast."

The smile was still there. What a handsome face it was. The bones beautifully modelled, the fair skin almost flawless, the complexion not too flushed. The blue scar across the bridge of his nose had faded many years ago, and the result of the accident which so nearly crushed that fine head was only to change the shape of his nose from being a straight one into a slightly aquiline one which lent a somewhat arrogant distinction to his expression. But what a shock it had been at the time. That was his only accident barring one other. I wondered how the long scar on his back looked now. That scar ran from the shoulder blade to the waist. It had been a scar across the whole family history. It had kept a good worker from his job for many weeks, and the growing family only just managed to live on his savings.

I wasn't born in those days, but I've often thought since how wise our old doctor had been to order Father to go to Eglwysilan, to the stream that chatters so gaily down the mountain slopes, and the little waterfall that tumbles into Cwmheldeg. My father was to strip naked there, the doctor had said, and bend his back beneath the cold stream, letting the water pound his muscles and make his back strong again. And so, the farm lad from Montgomeryshire would set his face towards the hills again, and having bowed before the exulting stream, look down into the valley at the tiny activities of the colliery below.

1948

41

ZULU WARRIOR

Gebuza Nungu

I am a Zulu born in Ulandi in 1870. My father was a witchdoctor, and so was my grandfather before him. My great-grandfather was Undabazimpi, a witch-doctor and chief, mentioned in one of Rider Haggard's books. My father came to England with King Cetewayo as prisoners after the Zulu War. Cetewayo was sent to St. Helena, but my father was allowed to return home. My father was commander of the Zulus who broke the British Square at Rorke's Drift. Our men surrounded the British soldiers in the middle of the night and fell upon them without them knowing.

When I was young it was my ambition to be a great chief like my father, and have lots of wives and cattle. I spent my early years with my brothers minding my father's cattle in my native village, but at an early age I drifted away.

In 1898 I came to England with "The Savage South Africa Show". I was twenty-eight. We came to Earl's Court Exhibition, and were there for six months. I was picked with other Zulus to appear in a command performance before the Prince of Wales, afterwards King Edward VII, and gave an exhibition of Zulu dancing and spear-throwing. When we finished at Earl's Court we went to the Paris Exhibition, but we didn't have a very good reception there, as we had killed their Prince Imperial. I saw him lying dead on the ground myself in 1879. He had been killed by our men when they broke the square at Rorke's Drift. Our men were feeling so happy because they thought they had killed a big man of England. They didn't know he was a Frenchman.

After "The Savage South Africa Show" broke up, Gebuza Nungu joined a circus. He left that for South Wales.

When I got out of the train at Llanelli, my first job was

to get lodgings. I walked along Station Road until I came to the town. Now the best place, I thought, to find out about lodgings would be a public house, so I went into the Cambrian Hotel in the middle of the town, and began asking the people in the bar. I noticed how they were all ready to help me, although I was a blackman. I was told to go to the cafe near the police station, but there, funnily enough, they refused to give me room. So I went to the police station to ask them if they could find me lodgings. A detective came across with me to the cafe and I had room. I stayed there a week then I went to lodge with a man I met at the cafe. Of course, I was now working in the Gorse galvanising works, and liking the work very much. When my wife came to Llanelli we went to live in Felinfoel, just outside the town. Though we were total strangers the people treated us as one of themselves. They used to bring us home-made tarts and, if they had been out shooting, woodcock and partridge.

My job at the Gorse works was a furnaceman, and I remember how disappointed the workmen were when they saw me sweating. They thought that because I came from Africa the heat would have no effect on me. Visitors when they came to the works always wanted to see working. They liked to see my great black body shining in the light of the fire, and watch the play of my muscles.

I remained at the Gorse for twenty-four years—the longest time I have ever stayed in one place. When I retired they made me a presentation, and I must say I felt it very deeply.

The Welsh people have always been very friendly to me and I have made some good pals among them. One day I was passing two little boys in the street, and one shouted afer me: "Blackman.". The other said, "That is not a blackman, that is Georgie Black"—the name I have been always known by in Llanelli.

1938

43

A BARREN LAND

DAN O'DRISCOLL

The one thing that made me choose Wales as my new home was the fact that I was—at 13—a keen politician. The chief topic in the house and the fields was Home Rule, and as I listened to the talk I realised that our only true support outside Ireland came from Wales. I read of Welsh Members of Parliament speaking and fighting in the House of Commons on behalf of Ireland, and there grew in me a bond of sympathy with these Welsh people who were ready to recognise the claims of my country.

I had a school-mate—a lad of my own age, named Dennis. He was in much the same position as myself. For a long time we talked and talked about getting away, but there came a day when I decided to do more than talk. "Dennis," says I, "I'm off."

"You are?" says he, "then I'm off with you. If one half of what these chaps say is true, then we'll be in clover."

A train to Cork and a boat to Milford, and the adventure had begun.

When we got to Swansea Station we had to decide where exactly we'd make for. Another school chum of mine had gone to Merthyr Vale and was working in the pits, and we thought we might as well look him up—it was a real comfort to know that there was *one* person in this strange land whom we knew well enough to call on—if we could find him.

While we waited for our train I had my first taste of Wales. We were a sociable pair of lads and anxious to get friendly with everybody. We got talking to a man on the platform, and as soon as it was decent we invited him to have one. Now 'porter' I was acquainted with, and when he said 'beer' I felt I was equal to it. I ordered three pints, and never shall I forget that first terrible mouthful. My mate and I looked at each other—"Dennis," says I, "We—very definitely—have left Ireland."

The journey to Merthyr Vale was a real eye-opener. I had never seen such a barren land. Whichever way I looked I saw nothing but bleak hillsides and great black tips. And I had left the green fields of Ireland for this! How could a man earn a living in a place where even the *grass* was fighting a losing battle?

The the train took a sudden turn, and I saw a large black patch, with low clouds of steam hanging over it. From the middle there rose a slender structure crowned with a huge wheel. All around there wagons filled with . . . Ah, so this was what a coal-mine looked like.

There was no need now to worry about those barren hillsides. You didn't plant corn in *this* soil. Your living lay deep in the bowels of the earth—that earth that I had been scratching with my plough.

1938

ANTONIO'S ICE-CREAM CART

Antonio Leonardi

A large number of people came to Wales from Bardi, a small village in Northern Italy, between the 1880's and 1920's. They established the Italian cafes that became famous throughout South Wales.

Now, it was the custom for certain natives of our village, who had gone to England to make their fortunes, to return home once every few years for a holiday. They looked so rich, walking about with gold and silver chains in their waistcoats, that they made me want to be like them. I really and truly thought at the time that gold could be picked up in the streets of England. These people, too, when they went back to England, used to take with them any boy who wanted to serve as an apprentice in their shops.

So when a neighbour of ours, who had a shop at Neath, came to visit us, I made up my mind to try my luck abroad, and go with him. I signed an agreement to stay with him for three years. I was then only fourteen years of age. My parents were unwilling for me to go, especially my mother, but my mind was made up.

The first thing I did when I stepped ashore in this country was to look on the ground for the golden sovereigns. I was very disappointed when I did not find any. My first wish was to go back to Italy, but that was impossible, because I had bound myself to my boss for three years, and, what is more, I had no money.

To make things worse, here was I in Wales knowing neither English nor Welsh. I might as well be deaf and dumb. You can guess how I felt, if you think of yourself in my country not knowing Italian. One thing I hated doing very much when I got to Neath, and that was going round the streets selling ice-cream.

I had always had the feeling that it was a common thing to do, and not a man's job. When I found I had to do it, I used to keep away from the main streets and go into the lanes and side-streets, because I didn't want people to see me.

When War broke out I served with my country and fought on the side of the Allies. At the end of the War I came back to this country and came to Llanelli. I came because I was offered a job there by one of my compatriots whom I served with in the army. I worked with him for eighteen months but found the hours very long.

While working there I noticed one customer who used to come to our shop very often for hot tea. She was a Welsh girl and able to speak English. I made up my mind, there and then, that she was a girl I was going to marry. But the trouble was how to get to know her. I had my chance one day when I saw her with a red rose in her coat. I made up my mind to ask her for it, but I thought that as I was of a different nationality she would snub me. I

46

remember her answer so well: "I'm sorry I can't give you this one, but I will bring you a bunch tomorrow." And she did. Sixteen months later she was my wife. Now she can speak Italian as well as Welsh and English.

1938

SPANISH ROOTS

Felepe Serrano

Felepe Serrano came from Bilbao to Dowlais to join a Spanish community already established there.

They thought we were dangerous people to bother with. They said we carried knives, and were only too glad of chance to use them. It is quite true that we are different from the Welsh people. We are quicker tempered—perhaps—and get very excited—sometimes—when we talk. But about the knives—that is all nonsense. The story started because of something that happened in Dowlais just before my family came over. Two Spaniards quarrelled, and one—so it was said—stabbed the other with a long . . . oh, *very* long . . . sharp knife. Of course, there was a great fuss, and well, the story started.

Now, that knife was *not* a knife. One of those men was a carpenter, and he used a file which he happened to be holding at the time. But you can't stop a story once it is started. In the end, the people of Dowlais found that we were a happy people. In a field near our houses at Penywern we gathered every evening and sang our songs to the music of guitars. Hundreds of Welsh people used to gather round and spend happy evenings with us.

But we are a shy people in a strange country, and we have not mixed much in the life of the town. Only those who came here very young and those born in Dowlais speak English very well. The older people—because they

47

do not mix—have found the language very difficult. Lots of Spanish children have been going to Dowlais chapels on Sundays, and one little Spanish girl, going to a Welsh Sunday School, passed out top of all in a written examination—in Welsh.

When I was a lad I mixed with everybody, and my best friend was a Welshman. He is my friend to-day, after over thirty years—and when I tell you that I married a Welsh girl, that should be enough to show how well I can get on with the Welsh people.

1938

RHONDDA

Gwyn Thomas

In any quick journey around the points of one's life, the points at which one knows that one has made a journey upon this earth, the one that will really stagger my mind will be the one that I saw in my early childhood, this massive revelation of human energy and geographical genius that shows the great dividing of the land into the big Rhondda Valley and the small.

Now, in the latter part of my life, when my sensibilities have become blunt, to say the least, I can still look upon this with a feeling of massive excitement. I can still feel the great movement of people coming from many parts of the world into these two narrow gulches, the sense of energy, the sense of absolute despair that so many human beings should have flooded into such narrow places and, indeed, not merely the narrow place of the valley, the hills almost within shouting distance of each other. You know, in places like Ynyshir people could conduct conversations from one side of the valley to another.

But actually they had to add to this complexity by leaving the surface of the earth and going underground.

48

This is what gives the majesty, the final touch, to the great irony of the Rhondda Valleys.

It is something unique, because it was uniquely monstrous in itself and you can't walk up and down these valleys at all without feeling these immense waves of sound that have come from the generations—not many generations you know—a very short experience the Rhondda.

They say that it is on the way out now. Of course every human thing is on the way out, but to see this thing that was once a great massive animal, because that's what it was, it was scarcely human in the scope of its energy, in the scope of its passion, in the scope of its talent, and there it lies now, you know, terribly wounded and all the rest of it.

Indeed, in my own life it took one peculiar form because as a very young boy my brother Emlyn, who had served in the Tank Corps in the First World War, (not to any great effect. He, as a pacifist, was very quick to inform us that he hadn't done much tanking but he had switched from tanks to music) had become a teacher of music in the Rhondda Valley of the early 1920s.

I can give you my own personal assurance that never in the history of this earth have there been so many people with the will and the ability to sing solo. They flooded into our front room as if they were a race of musical lemmings. Night after night new recruits would come. And why was this? Because I think that there was something so volcanic about the social experience of the Rhondda and similar mining valleys that people had this absolute compulsion to be lyrical, to be expressive, to leave some kind of expression of what they felt upon this earth. Some did it through politics, but the great mass did it through a desire to be musical; and the number of singers that I have heard in that front room who simply sang what they thought was a possible chance of entry into the great world of professional music were simply singing a kind of lament

49

for the whole world of the Rhondda Valley that had been begotten with such hope and such beauty.

But they, like the Rhondda Valley itself, couldn't really keep in tune. The lower part of the Rhondda Valley and that astonishing ridge, so harsh, rocky, threatening—it should have kept the place secure for eons but, of course, we didn't realise the ingenuity or the diabolical cleverness of men. And the place was overcome and despoiled and totally humiliated.

1980

BUTETOWN

Betty Campbell

In the past, Butetown was a very thriving port and wherever you have a port, you have sailors, and wherever you have sailors, you have houses of ill-repute and I think that was one of the reasons why Butetown had a bad name. And then there were stories of violence and the policemen used to walk down Bute Street in twos and threes. But despite the identification that Butetown has had outside the area, I don't think there's one person in the world who would be ashamed to say, "I was born in Butetown."

1984

Olwen Watkins

Butetown to me is *the* place, it's ace, it's whatever, it's the place to be, it's the place to live, the place to die. I'll go anywhere in the world as long as I've got a return ticket. It's warm, it's full of love and it's great. It's not the look of the place really, it's just the feeling of the tolerance, this

50

love that permeates, there are always hands reaching out
to help. We could gladly show some places in this world
how people can get on together across religions and races
and live in a happy, harmonious kind of way. It bring tears
to my eyes.

1984

LINDA MITCHELL

Tears and laughter—that sums up life in Cardiff's dockland
suburb Butetown. Its residents know nothing about the
grey mediocrity of other inner-city areas. When life here
is bad, it's bad. When it's good, it's memorable. Why else
should people like Betty Campbell and Olwen Watkins
decide to stay. Born and brought up in the area, like my
mother, they remember the pleasures and delights of
their childhood. Mixing with children of all races, faiths
and backgrounds. They realise what really matters in
relations with others. Black and white living together,
suffering together and worshipping together. They learnt
about integration before it became fashionable.

1984

MERTHYR TYDFIL

LESLIE NORRIS

Merthyr was a great place really for a boy to grow up I
think. It was a sad town of course, in the Twenties and
Thirties, but wonderful for boys. It was full of great
characters. Children were valued in that place for some
odd reason. And I was very fortunate in that I spent a lot
of time on the farm outside the town, which was a family
farm. My grandfather had been born there, and *his* father,

and I spent weeks and weeks and months and months there. If a child can have a conception of heaven and hell, I had as near as a little boy can get to it in that there was an ideal heaven of the country farm, with its mixed animals and birds in the one huge field around the house, and its pond; and then the mean streets through which I walked to school, and unemployed men on the corners of the streets and the cold weather. In fact I believe that, sometime during the years I was growing up, a Royal Commission coming to Merthyr in the very worst weather of the winter, gave as its serious logical con-clusion that the town should be pulled down and all of us re-housed on the banks of the Severn somewhere. Well we wouldn't have liked that. Around the town it was incredibly beautiful. And so I knew early on. I had concrete evidence early on of the difference between the ideal and the hellish.

1983

ABERDOVEY

BERTA RUCK

Excitement galore filled those winters of the eighties, when we spent Christmas holidays with Nain by the sea at Aberdovey. Was it only because I was a child that it seemed a place so out of this world? On the one hand high hill-sides where, even in December, you could find golden gorse blossoms. On the other hand the sea, and the sun going red into the waves. It was, anyhow, still a busy little port, with plenty going on.

The old wooden pier was my favourite haunt; delightful terror of seeing through cracks between the planks on which I walked, sea-water washing far below! The thrill of staring up at the visiting sailing-ships and their intriguing figure-heads, carved and colourfully painted ladies in balldress bodices, some with gilded crowns on their wavy tresses, and lettered on the ship's side their names— *Mary Davies* and *The Star of Hope.*

I seem to remember those winters of the eighties being always full of sunshine. But I also remember exhilarating cold frosty days that turned the flooded marsh into a two mile stretch of black and perfect ice. On this my father, his brothers and nephews skated and cut figures of eight. Top thrill was when they quarried out a thick slab of ice, cushioned it with marsh rushes, bored a hole for a rope to go through and lo! a magnificent sledge. Our mother with her face pink as a rose, startled, delighted, holding us children in turn on her lap, was whizzed along like the wind. Only my first flight in an open aeroplane has meant such ecstasy!

1957

YSTRADGYNLAIS

JOSEF HERMAN

The miner is the man of Ysytradgynlais.

Already in his appearance, although at first sight alike to other workers, the miner is more impressive and singular.

Sometimes I thought of old Egyptian carvings walking between sky and earth, or dark rocks fashioned into glorious human shapes, or heavy logs in which a primitive hand has tried to synthesize the pride of human labour and the calm force which promise to guard its dignity.

It would be true to say that the miner is the walking monument of labour.

By this singularity of appearance, amid the clean figures of the shopkeepers, the thin and tall figures of the town councillors, the robust figures of the insurance agents, the respectable figures of the ministers, and the fatigued figures of the schoolmasters, the miners form, like trees among vegetables, a solid group.

But what makes a group so singular outside is but the strong similarity within the group.

Like the houses with doors smaller than men, like the two china dogs on the mantlepiece, like the taste of the blackberry tart, they are similar in each house.

The kind of mauve scarf and the way they wear it; the manner of nodding their heads sideways in greeting, the feeling of relief and comfort they express as they stride in the middle of the road, the way of sitting near a wall and supporting their bodies with the heel of the foot.

Similar are also the troubles and joys.

What happens to-day to one happens tomorrow to another. Therefore there is sincere concern in each others lives, and duties become habits.

Men must give each other a hand. Familiarity breaks the ice of strangeness.

"You're no stranger here"—I was told the very day I arrived. A day later I was addressed as "Joe," and now I am nicknamed "Joe bach,"—"little Joe."

If someone more individualistically-tempered does not like the familiarity, people here will easily find this out, and even the dogs won't bark after him.

Men need each other if only to talk to—or just to make the heart easier.

Thus men listen with heavy concentration, and share feelings, laughter, tears.

Birth or death are faced as a matter of fact, the first without too much fuss, the other without too much gloom. But the unexpected is encountered with gravity.

One afternoon a little street was empty but for a few dogs walking here and there.

The two rows of houses and the black road between them were in a peaceful light.

An old man, bent like a walking stick with his head

hanging down on his chest, was knocking at a door, then at another door, and so door after door, door after door.

At every door he spent but a moment.

A woman or man or the two together came to the open door, listen to the old man, some take the apron to their eyes, others just nod sadly.

When he came nearer to me I thought that evening that Welsh must be the only language of music, of sorrow.

He had lost his son in the Far East.

Then on the Teddy Bear Bridge I met three pregnant women. Their shapes were enormous and of unearthly beauty. Near them all Venuses would look but pale girls. Walt Whitman looking at them would repeat his psalm-sounding phrase: "And I say there is nothing greater than mother of man."

The three mothers of man talked of death.

The whole village talked of death.

1945

VALLEYS

IDRIS DAVIES

These valleys are not all colliery-sidings and slag-heaps and crooked streets. There are pleasant places among the hillsides, and there is some variety of scenery, especially when you cross from one valley into another. And, of course, communication is easy in the valleys. You are neither far from the Severn Sea to the south, nor from the mountains of Breconshire to the north. We who were born in these valleys know too well that our homes are not among the beautiful places of the earth, but we have, nevertheless, a shrewd idea that there are worse places in the world to live in.

After all, it is not so much the landscape itself that matters. The essence of the thing is often in its associations.

Even the old slag-heaps themselves are more than mere slag-heaps to some of us. They are for ever associated with generations of our people who gave so much of their blood and sweat in the years gone by. And at present we unconsciously feel that they are part and parcel of our daily lives. Perhaps, some day, the valleys that once were so wild and green and very beautiful will become wild and beautiful again, with all the ravages of industrialism hidden and forgotten under the blossoming trees of far-off summers. But that will come to pass only when we and all our tumult are gone and utterly forgotten.

We live today and not in the far future. Most of us live a little in the past, too. For me there is one very dear place among these mining valleys. It is a part of the hillside overlooking the town of Rhymney, for it was there on one cloudless summer afternoon, on a grassy ridge near the Gnoll Farm, that I read the poetry of Shelley for the first time.

The words seemed to dazzle with colour and music as I lay there in the full blaze of the sun, with the mountain grasses quivering, hardly quivering in the breeze of the afternoon. Not far below me were the streets and the pitheads sweltering in the June sunshine, and an occasional echo from the colliery-surface would break through the air. But there was I, almost oblivious of all other things, reading Shelley for the first time in my life. Do you wonder that I think of that hillside above my home as a piece of sacred ground?

1943

SWANSEA

Vernon Watkins

I like to think of Swansea as a place with no sophistication, no cultural props, no reputation of any kind. A hidden place. Compressed as it is between the bay, which people have so often compared with the Bay of Naples, and its own seven hills, and urged from within by its so-called improvers, it has only with difficulty preserved its character. The levellers and planners have achieved much, but they have not overcome the stubborn oddity of the town. Nothing can take away the steep incline of Constitution Hill, with its rail to assist pedestrians to the top. Here they can watch it swaying over the sea, balancing the residential streets on either side like a tightrope-walker. The grass of the Recreation Ground can never compete with the boots that play on it. Brynmill Park still holds its collection of incongruous cages. Cwmdonkin Park is as it was when Dylan Thomas wrote his poem *The Hunchback in the Park*, except that the reservoir is dry; it seems just as it was when I played in it as a child.

The lake of Singleton survives, undisturbed, the activities of builders. St. Helen's cricket ground is greener than ever. There are more policemen, but walls are still climbed, and cricket matches are watched from houses with vulnerable windows and the railway bridge.

Oysters have gone from the bay, as well as from South-end, between Oystermouth and the Mumbles Pier, where they used to be packed high in barrels of seaweed. But at low tide, when the bay is a waste of wet mud, stakes and shreds of nets are still visible. The hill above the pier has been cut and its contour altered by progress and excavations, but the rock on which the lighthouse stands is the same as when Landor saw it, and so is the surrounding coast-line, the one picture on which he longed to look when he was an exile in Italy.

Of the town's old shopping centre hardly a trace remains: it was burnt to the ground early in 1941. When the old buildings were down and before the new were erected, the hills could be seen clearly from the centre, and there was room for an amphitheatre in the rubble. Where once was variegated congestion, after an empty interval of open ground, there is now uniform pressure, and the streets are more crowded than ever before. Much that we value is under the auctioneer's hammer. There is an open market that is about to close, a closed market that has just opened, a big theatre that is gone, and a little theatre that is coming again. The two old dredgers, the Flea and the Bug, rot in the dockyard, while Swansea assimilates and reproduces its violent yet identical changes like the sea.

1961

PICTUREGOERS

JOHN ORMOND

When cinematography was being invented down in Brighton by William Friese-Greene, another system was being devised by a man called Rudge. It didn't survive, the more's the pity. It was called the Bio-Phantoscope, and it's the perfect name to go with the Carlton, and the rest of the litany of Swansea cinemas which were (and some of them are still there today) The Plaza, The Rialto, The Elysium, The Castle, The Albert Hall, The Palace, The Maxime, if you please. How many Regals were there in South Wales? Aberdare had its Coliseum; and it also had its Rex (owned, incidentally, by the Willis family whose famous son played inside-half for Wales, but whether the cinema was named after the son, or the son after the cinema, I can't tell you). Llanelli had its Ritz (though come to think of it perhaps that was a ballroom). Then

JOSEFF HERMAN

BBC Wales

DYLAN THOMAS

BBC Hulton Picture Library

there were the Capitols, Hippodromes and Palladiums. And the Tivolis.

My first Tiv was in Gowerton, the next village to ours (the Lido was all the way over in Gorseinon, and the Adelphi light-years away in Burry Port). The thing with the Gowerton Tiv was that the show always ended at half-past-nine and the last bus home went at ten-past-nine. Which meant that until I was about twelve I never once saw the *end* of any *single* film which accounts, I suppose, for my neurosis and my feeling that the world in general is an incomplete sort of place.

Although the Empire (next door to the Carlton in Swansea), that was all right; a music-hall with gold cherubs and angels and chandeliers and red plush. The chief commissionaire there had enough gold braid on him to keep four or five admirals going. His name was Mr. Penny, but you had to slip him sixpence for him to get you a ticket ahead of the queue. And up in The Gods the man who kept order was a Mr. Cyclino, a former stage turn himself, who once a year cycled from outside Swansea Jail to the Mumbles, *backwards*.

I went back to have a look at The Carlton again a couple of days ago. There are pot-bellied cherubs on the Carlton, too. They are in not-so-pot-bellied bas-relief, four rectangular panels in grey and dirty stone (it would soon clean up) and on the left they are running about with sticks and bunches of grapes. On the right they have been joined by a seventh. They are playing some game which is partly tug-of-war and partly tearing up the contents of a laundry-basket, and the poor seventh cherub is being laid low by a professional foul.

There's a smashing (though perhaps that's not the way to describe a window) piece of glass-work, centrally. It resembles one of those domes you find placed over stuffed-foxes or ormolu clocks; but in this case it's been pushed into the face of the building. And, on the top, a balustrade, a rather dumpy Swan-Lake-type balustrade,

I'm afraid. And, above that, a kind of Parthenon-pigeon-loft, two pinnacles with holes-in, heavy with stone wreaths that (if they were really flowers) would do for you, good and proper, if they were placed above your neck, albeit in welcome, in Hawaii. It's all a bit like the decor, in stone, of the Queen Mary (the liner, I mean, not the queen) turned inside-out. But good.

I saw King Kong in The Carlton . . . 1933 . . . I fancied Fay Wray rather more than King Kong; but, then, most of my sex and inclination and generation *did*.

There aren't many Dylan Thomas stories left unreported. But, again, my guess is, that this is one of them. He loved Westerns, but generally went by the titles. Confused and misled, one wet Thursday afternoon, by some such title as *Desert Hotspot*, he went into the Carlton. There were already as many as four or five people in the audience. The film wasn't about the Wild West at all. It was about the white-slave trade, and a beautiful blonde girl (a bit like Fay Wray I imagine) was being auctioned in an Eastern bazaar.

The price of the girl, the bidding, went up and up. It reached a crisis. The crackly silence on the soundtrack grew longer between the bids.

". . . Will no-one offer me more than five thousand pieces of gold?

(crackle-crackle on the soundtrack)

". . . This exquisite, wild creature . . . (a *big* close-up)

". . . Is she to be sold for a paltry a sum? Will nobody bid more?"

Suddenly there was a loud cry from the small auditorium. It was Dylan Thomas, on his feet, as surprised as any by the sound of his own voice, as he shouted, "I will, I will."

1980

60

RETURN JOURNEY

DYLAN THOMAS

Narrator: It was a cold white day in High Street, and nothing to stop the wind slicing up from the Docks, for where the squat and tall shops had shielded the town from the sea there lay their blitzed flat graves marbled with snow and headstoned with fences. Dogs, delicate as cats on water, as though they had gloves on their paws padded over the vanished buildings. Boys romped, calling high and clear, on top of a levelled chemists and a shoe-shop, and a little girl, wearing a man's cap, threw a snowball in a chill deserted garden that had once been the Jug and Bottle of the Prince of Wales. The wind cut up the street with a soft sea-noise hanging on its arm, like a hooter in a muffler. I could see the swathed hill stepping up out of the town, which you never could see properly before, and the powdered fields of the roofs of Milton Terrace and Watkin Street and Fullers Row. Fishfrailed, netbagged, umbrella'd pixie-capped, fur-shoed, blue-nosed, puce-lipped, blinkered like drayhorses, scarved, mittened, goloshed, wearing everything but the cat's blanket, crushes of shopping women crunched in the little Lapland of the once grey drab street, blew and queued and yearned for hot tea, as I began my search through Swansea town cold and early on that wicked February morning.

I went into the hotel.

"Good morning."

The hall-porter did not answer. I was just another snowman to him. He did not know that I was looking for someone after fourteen years, and he did not care. He stood and shuddered, staring through the glass of the hotel door at the snowflakes sailing down the sky like Siberian confetti. The Bar was just opening, but already one customer puffed and shook at the counter with a full pint of half-frozen Tawe water in his wrapped-up hand. I said Good morning, and the barmaid, polishing the counter as vigourously as though it were a rare and valuable piece of Swansea china, said to her first customer:

Barmaid: Seen the film at the Elysium Mr. Griffiths there's snow isn't it did you come up on your bicycle our pipes burst Monday . . .

Narrator: A pint of bitter, please.

Barmaid: Proper little lake in the kitchen got to wear your wellingtons when you boil a egg one and four please . . .

Customer: The cold gets me just by here . . .

Barmaid: . . . and eightpence change that's your liver Mr. Griffiths you been on the cocoa again . . .

Narrator: I wonder whether you remember a friend of mine. He always used to come to this bar, some years ago. Every morning, about this time.

Customer: Just by here it gets me. I don't know what'd happen if I didn't wear a band . . .

Barmaid: What's his name?

Narrator: I said: Young Thomas.

Barmaid: Lots of Thomases come here it's a kind of home from home for Thomases isn't it Mr. Griffiths what's he look like?

Narrator: (slowly) He'd be about seventeen or eighteen . . .

Barmaid: . . . I was seventeen once . . .

Narrator: . . . and above medium height. Above medium height for Wales, I mean, he's five feet six and a half. Thick blubber lips; snub nose; curly mousebrown hair; one front tooth broken after playing a game called cats and dogs in the Mermaid, Mumbles; speaks rather fancy; truculent; plausible; a bit of a shower-off; plus fours and no breakfast, you know; used to have poems printed in the Herald of Wales, there was one about an open-air performance of Electra in Mrs. Berti Perkins' garden in Sketty; lived up the Uplands; a bombastic adolescent provincial bohemian with a thick-knotted artist's tie made out of his sister's scarf, she never knew where it had gone, and a cricket-shirt dyed bottle-green; a gabbing, ambitious, mock-tough, pretentious young man; and mole-y, too.

1947

ABERFAN

Gwyn Thomas

Of all the disasters that have struck Wales none has caused more anguish and bitterness than that of Aberfan in October 1966. Industrial history swept down on small children as, without warning, a mountain of coal waste engulfed a primary school. One hundred and forty four people died—one hundred and sixteen of them children.

Before this event we stand breathless. Our eyes speak, our thoughts rage, but our tongues have momentarily given up the ghost of immemorial grievance. No touch of the whip has hurt quite like this. In these bare, forlorn villages the schools are the most beautiful of communities. They are the living emblem of everybody's hope; there the children make their way towards a world that would be remade in the new light of new understanding. Never have I known such deep creative comradeship between teacher and taught as in those places. It is a conscious crusade to heal the old wounds and demand a reasonable restitution of life, a reign of gentleness for which the children of those twisted streets had probably been praying in their assembly hall a few minutes before they were engulfed. At the beginning of an hour there was in that school a union of men, women and children in a simple act of knowledge and love. At the end of that hour there was a black indignity of silence and death.

63

There are still many who give too little thought to the value and the welfare of the young, the young who belong to no region, to no time, who are without innocence or guilt, who are the common property and the common pride of the whole world. And there are those too little conscious of the problem of unpleasant and unprivileged places.

They will do well to think of the young scholars of Aberfan who will never sing in their little assembly hall again, never nourish their minds in classrooms again for the enjoyment of a better earth. We mourn today in order to further that hope.

1967

ABERFAN II

VINCENT KANE

Once more in these last autumn weeks I have been making the journey from Cardiff up the valley to Aberfan, a path I've trodden many times in twenty years, returning each time with my mood fashioned by what I had seen and heard. Horror at first and stupefaction; then choking grief followed by a bottomless sorrow, and after that anger and recrimination, resentment, exasperation and finally, as the years followed each other, resignation. Well, wait a moment. Is that the prevailing mood? Are the people of Aberfan resigned and at peace with the disaster which tore their community apart twenty years ago? What would the visitor or the returning exile find today?

Perhaps the most significant thing is what he would not find. The tips—they are gone. Look up from the floor of these Welsh valleys and the skyline is clear. Those black brooding giants of slurry and slag and coal dust on which nothing would grow and under whose shadow so many Welsh children played and grew up have been removed.

And not only in Aberfan but from scores of other sites in industrial and post-industrial Wales where the tip lingered on often long after the mining activity had ceased as a legacy, an eyesore and a blot on the landscape. Aberfan quickened the pace of land reclamation in Wales.

So the tips are gone; so is the old primary school, of course, demolished by that wall of slurry. In its place a memorial garden and an open space where today's generation of eight, nine and ten year olds play happily, safely and without inhibition. It was those three years, the three top forms of the primary school which were wiped out twenty years ago, and for the very few survivors of that age group growing up in Aberfan has been an empty, friendless experience.

I spoke to one such last week. Elizabeth, who was eight at the time—her ten year old brother was killed—had just slipped out of class to pay her dinner money when the avalanche came down. She was buried but rescued hours later and spent two years in and out of hospital.

She told me that as a teenager, she had been terribly lonely and had imagined that when she left school she would leave Aberfan. But when the time came she couldn't. She felt compelled to stay, as did virtually all the bereaved parents.

That I find truly remarkable, for Aberfan was a depressing, unprivileged place and when the monies from the Aberfan Appeal Fund, which provoked so much rage and controversy that it was called the Second Disaster, were finally shared among the bereaved, there was five thousand pounds each, which nearly twenty years ago was a sum easily sufficient for a family to start again elsewhere. But they didn't. Instead they refurbished and extended and equipped their homes and brightened them so that the streets of Aberfan are no longer shabby and mean and with the residue of the fund they built the Aberfan

Community Centre with an Olympic size swimming pool, games room, committee rooms and bars.

The home-comer's trip to Aberfan will probably end as mine did—at the most important landmark of all. The children's cemetery overlooking the town where they all lie side by side. Standing there I recalled that the Aberfan disaster was as the Tribunal of Inquiry clearly ruled not an act of God or a bolt from the blue, but a man-made disaster, caused by greed and negligence.

Greed to mine as much coal for our energy needs as we could, without caring too much about the waste products— and it occurred to me in this year of Chernobyl, when who knows how many innocent people will again perish as a result of man's search for energy, that the lesson of Aberfan is that in our pursuit of warmth and heat and light we still owe a duty of care to each other, and between communities, and between nations.

When we ignore that duty the world caves in, as it did in Aberfan twenty years ago.

1986

TWO NATIONS

HARRY SOAN

In the spring of 1932 our first child died. By the autumn we felt we had better go away, and see if a change of scene would help to change our frame of mind. So in September we packed a tent into the car and went. Quite without plans, we found ourselves wandering across Hereford-shire, into Radnor, then on to Montgomery, Merioneth and Caernarvon. It was our first visit to Wales. The scenery attracted us and somehow gave us quieter minds than we had known for months.

On a calm evening we turned back into Merioneth to Bala, across the lakehead into Cwm Hirnant, intending to go over the rough pass to Lake Vyrnwy. As we were passing the last farm up, Maes-y-fallen, an old man stopped us and in broken English bade us go no further, because it was too late to travel by so bad a road. We spent that night in one of his fields, and the next day we went home, acquainted with Wales, liking it uncommonly well and vowing we'd return and know it better.

We came back every year, till the war broke out, and always to the old man's valley, till we knew every twist of the river and every cleft in the surrounding hills. Always too, to the same people—but of them knowledge came slowly. At first the Roberts, who occupied the farm, were no more than courteous; but in time they became more welcoming and would prepare the house and lay in firewood for us. They allowed us to do small messages for them in the town and to help at the hay-making. Eventually we became friends—nothing was ever said, but we knew it. Evan Roberts and his wife and brother would come of an evening for tea and talk round the fire.

The gamekeeper and his wife made us free of Dolwen-Isa and in time Cwm Hirnant became a second home to us.

What did we think of the Welsh? Certainly their strange language, peculiar ways, their ready hospitality and their unfeigned delight in plain human intercourse contrasted strangely to the more sophisticated life we lived. It was, obviously, a tenacious survival of an ancient life, and to our superficial observation its survival was due more to geography than to the quality of a culture. But for those mountains life there, we thought, would have been indistinguishable from that of rural England.

We returned from our 1939 holiday the day before war was declared and we didn't know when, if ever, our connection with Wales would be resumed. But two years later we had the opportunity to come and live in Wales—West Wales—and unhesitatingly we took it. Had we known then what we know now we should still have come but not unhesitatingly. Had we thought then we should have said: "Live in Wales? Why not? We can live our English lives as well in Wales as in England." Today we know that that is not the case. Again, we should have said: "The language? What of that? The Welsh all speak English." But we overlooked the fact that we are an argumentative couple and can't stay as long on the subject of the weather as some people can. Consequently, the Welsh language was a barrier, like a polar region between us and the life of the neighbourhood. For five years we have lived as in a glass prison, able to see and be seen but not to communicate freely. It has given us a sense of being foreigners here, though not without good friends. And because the isolation has been real it has been painful. I've been at shearings, handing out cording or carrying out sheep all day, and apart from calls for cording or carrier few words have been spoken to me. It has happened at funerals too, when I've felt that by an unfortunate mistake the wrong corpse had got into the coffin. At times the isolation has been grim and sometimes we have wondered how we would fare if serious sickness overtook us. So these five years have been like a long frost, and although the thaw is beginning I fancy the lesson of it will remain. The lesson that the Welsh and the English are not one people but two. The lesson that Wales is not just a peculiar corner of England, but a distinct part of Britain, the home of the Welsh nation.

There, it seems to me, lies the explanation of the Welshmen who didn't fit in to English life. They didn't because they couldn't. Different histories have bred us, different cultures have nurtured us, and therefore subtle but real differences mark us off from each other.

We believe, however, that these differences need divide us only if they are ignored.

The Welsh and the English are distinct peoples, and no good can come of not recognising this. Given the opportunity to know and understand each other in the light of our histories there is no reason why we two peoples shouldn't live together in mutual goodwill and co-operation.

1947

QUITE EARLY ONE MORNING

DYLAN THOMAS

The town was not yet awake. The milkman lay still, lost in the clangour and music of their Welsh spoken dreams, the wishfulfilled tenor voices, more powerful than Caruso's, sweeter than Ben Davies's, thrilling past Cloth Hall and Manchester House up to the frosty hills.

The town was not yet awake. Babies, in upper bedrooms of salt white houses dangling over water or of bow-windowed villas squatting prim in neatly treed but unsteady hill-streets, worried the light with their half-in-sleep cries. Miscellaneous retired sea captains emerged for a second from deeper waves than ever tossed their boats, then drowned again, going down, down into a perhaps Mediterranean-blue cabin of sleep rocked to the sea-beat of their years. Landladies, shawled and bloused and aproned with sleep, in the curtained bombazine-black of their once-spare-rooms, remembered their loves, their bills, their visitors dead, decamped, or buried in English deserts till the trumpet of next expensive August roused them again to the world of holiday rain, dismal cliff and sand seen through the weeping windows of front parlours, tasselled tablecloths, stuffed pheasants, ferns in pots, fading photographs of the bearded and censorious dead, autograph albums with a look of limp and colourless beribboned hair lolling out between the thick, black boards.

The town was not yet awake. Birds sang in caves, bushes, trees, on telegraph wires, rails, fences, spars and wet masts, not for love or joy but to keep other birds away: the landlords in feathers disputed the right of even the flying light to descend and perch.

The town was not yet awake, and I walked through the streets like a stranger come out of the sea, shrugging off weed and wave and darkness with each step, or like an inquisitive shadow determines to miss nothing: not the preliminary tremor in the throat of the dawn-saying cock or the first whirring nudge of arranged time in the belly of the alarm clock on the trinketted chest-of-drawers under the knitted text and the done-by-hand water colours of Porthcawl or Trinidad.

I walked past the small sea-spying windows behind whose trim curtains lay mild-mannered men and women not yet awake and, for all I could know, terrible and violent in their dreams. In the head of Miss Hughes the Cosy clashed the cymbals of an Eastern Court, eunuchs struck gongs the size of Bethesda Chapel, sultans with voices fiercer than visiting preachers demanded a most unWelsh dance; everywhere there glowed and rayed the colours of the small slate-grey woman's dreams: purple, magenta, ruby, sapphire, emerald, vermilion, honey. But I could not believe it. She knitted in her tidy sleepworld a beige woollen shroud, with "Thou Shalt Not" on the bosom. I could not imagine Cadwalladar Davies the grocer, in his near-to-waking dream, riding on horseback, two-gunned and Cody-bold, through the cactused prairies: he added, he subtracted, he receipted, he filed a prodigious account, with a candle dipped in dried egg. What big seas of dreams ran in the captain's sleep? Over what blue-whaled waves did he sail through a rainbow-hail of flying fishes to the music of Circe's swinish island? Do not let him be dreaming of dividends and bottle beer and onions.

Someone was snoring in one house: I counted ten savagely indignant grunt-and-groans, like those of a pig in a model and mudless farm, which ended with a window-rattler, a washbasin-shaker, a trembler of toothglasses, a waker of dormice. It thundered with me up to the chapel railings, then brassily vanished.

The chapel stood grim and grey, telling the day there was to be no nonsense. The chapel was not asleep; it never cat-napped nor nodded nor closed its long, cold eye. I left it telling the morning off, and a seagull hung, rebuked, above it.

1945

GRITTY, GUSTY TOWNS

DR. BERTHA HALL

There is a dignity in fine industrial plant but there is none in the deadly monotony of miners' houses pressing close upon one another in the colourless industrial towns. Small and cramped at times, seeming to balance perilously on narrow shelves they betray the meanness of men who deemed such a setting fit for humans. In these colourless, gritty, gusty towns, the psalmist has more than once come to my mind, "I will lift up mine eyes unto the hills"—for there above all the drabness and squalor are the golden slopes. Climbing rapidly up the hard, steep road in a small town one day I found myself laughingly warned by a home-going miner: "Try a lower gear, lady."

From a physical point of view his advice struck me as very sound, but I longed to reply: "No, friend! Try a higher gear and speed up your fellow men so that they exclaim—this and this must go: for our young life we demand space, beauty and convenience in our homes."

As a Londoner, I miss my garden and the joy of flowers around me. Why are so few flowers cultivated in South Wales, for instance? I have looked too in vain for the artist's hand. With a few outstanding exceptions the towns are unlovely: shops seem to lack the touch of those who understand the beauty of materials and other man-made things: they jostle one another: there is no tranquility, spaciousness or sense of design. And yet travel on a bus top and you may be rewarded by beauty of another kind. The other day I found myself surrounded by a group of tinplate workers who had scarcely seated themselves before they broke into song and the road lost its ugliness in the beauty of sound.

Waiting in a station buffet for a belated train one day I found myself quietly carried back to Covent Garden Opera in peace time. A small group of Welsh soldiers were softly singing strains from *Aida*. I asked them why, with such beauty within them, the men of Wales had not built beauty around. "We haven't the driving force" one replied: " 'Tomorrow will do' is largely our motto."

1941

CITY EYES

JOHN PETTS

After six months' probation in the liferooms, I gained my studentship at the Royal Academy Schools in London, holding in my hand at last that coveted 'ivory', the name-engraved plaque presented to each student, just like the ones held in the hands of William Blake, John Millais, Turner and many other young artists.

A mixed bag, the students, from far and wide, and a noticeably talkative and lively group came from Wales, lightening the gloom of the schools' corridors with their singing voices. 'Ighly-strung', was the comment of one of the porters, 'Ighly-strung, like bloody 'arps!'. There was tall Fred Jones from Swansea, his head full of theories, Bromfield Rees, his lean and studious friend from Llanelli, trying to paint like Braque, and the ubiquitous South Wales bonhomie was heightened by the frequent calling of black-bearded Mervyn Levy from the Royal College of Art, and a pudgy, fag-ended young journalist in a cocky-pork-pie hat and a dyed-green shirt whose name was Dylan Thomas. But the rare person to me, as she walked softly down the flagged corridor, was a short, slip of a golden-haired girl, tripping lightly like a young nun in her sandals and long, white overall, ever smiling, with a long, aquiline head like Lawrence of Arabia: this was Brenda Chamberlain from Bangor in North Wales.

As I grew to know her, it seemed that her whole small being was lit with pure delight, delight in the beauty and mystery of those aspects of the created world she loved, most especially the mountains of Eryri, the dramatic landscape of Snowdonia . . . and, my word, how she *did* know the ridges, rivers and lakes of that wild region, having explored it since girlhood.

Came the long summer vacation, and, committed to a full programme of holiday study, we rented a shepherd's cottage high in the hills above Aber in Gwynedd. Truly, I shall never forget the first impact of that landscape. The train from Euston dropped me at Aber Station, on the flatlands by the sea.

Across the water rested the whaleback of Puffin Island, off the point of the wide Isle of Anglesey, *Mam Cymru*, the Mother of Wales, called so since she fed the country from her golden cornlands in ancient days. The road led up into the hills above the wooded valley through which the river tumbled from the silver falls. Steadily I climbed up a steep side-track, leaving the trees behind, climbing to the open mountain with its tussocks of gorse and fine, sheep-bitten turf. The hills unfolded beyond; all was magically soaked in subtle greens and duns, patterned with grey rocks and screes, and all sang with the splendour of the clear light, and its voice was the cry of distant sheep and the fall of water. My city eyes were astounded, and my heart was singing.

Along the hill, and there was the cottage, tucked under the slope like a lamb under her dam. Above it spread a wide poplar tree, surprising to see in such a tree-less place, and there was Brenda smiling at the door. "The kettle's boiling . . ." she said. Sharing life with her was participating in a special sacrament. That simple little house where we slept on hay and cooked on a pungent fire of gorse twigs under the wide chimney, was my first home in Wales. For us its name was full of special meaning; *Hafod y Gelyn*, the Summer Shelter from the Enemy.

Subsequently, with our studentship ending in London, and impatient with the meaningless arguments and affectations of the art world, since art to us was part of religion, and disgusted now by all the flattery and wheeler-dealing of the commercial Bond Street galleries, we fled back to our own reality in Wales. We found two derelict cottages side by side, with a quarter of an acre of land, on the mountain-side above Llanllechid, near Bethesda, at the gateway to Snowdonia,—and all for £68, freehold.

From the front door you could look down over the Menai Straits across thirty miles of Anglesey. In winter snowstorms mountain ponies sheltered against the back wall. Our aim now, out on our own, 'doing our own thing' as later became the fashionable phrase, was to live by our art, willy-nilly, from hand to mouth, grow some of our own food, gather wood for the fire. Years later, looking back, Brenda described us in one of her books as 'the first hippies in Wales', but I don't relish the term. Rather I'd say that we were 'bread-I-dip-in-the-river' young Romantics.

1983

JOHN PETTS

JACK JONES

BBC Wales

CAPITAL CITY

Dr. Thomas Jones

Why bother about a capital? If Wales had had a capital, writes W. J. Gruffydd, we'd have had a National Theatre. Perhaps. How long has it taken London? Do we need a capital to demonstrate the Welsh way of life? Will Cardiff do that? And what is that Welsh way? Is it definable? Is it exportable? Is it to be found in Patagonia? Is it a way of service or of dominion? Is its centre of gravity in this world or the next? Is it inseparable from the language? Is its genius confined to a literature? Does it mean hymn singing on the football field on Saturday and public houses closed on Sunday?

Is the provision of a capital the remedy for our troubles? No. Their root is in the moral confusion of the time. We are witnessing the funeral of a culture which no longer commands allegiance. Our Welsh way was a rural way; it knew nothing of rayon factories in the north, nothing of nylon factories in the south. Can we substitute an Anglo-Welsh culture?

Today you can order an administrative capital by post from London. It is already arriving in instalments in the shape of regional offices for Education, Health, Town and Country Planning, Hospital Board, Gas Board. If this makes for convenience because Cardiff is only three hours from London, then I should proclaim Cardiff the administrative capital of Wales. But you can't obtain a cultural capital by post. Rather, I would say, let it be the town in which the perambulating National Eisteddfod meets annually. The permanent cultural capital will tend to be where the nation's books are. They arrive at Aberystwyth by the ton. One of the four petitions tells us that the Roman Empire, at its peak, stretched from the Persian Gulf to Caernarvon. The books we have at the National Library if placed end to end would stretch from Aberystwyth to the Persian Gulf.

1951

75

UNDERGROUND

Prysor Williams

Down, down, down, or was it up, up, up? Men, bumps, brattice, horses, rails, ropes, black faces, hauliers shouting a long panorama of ghostly figures. Who can't forget the first impression that a colliery makes on his mind? From 7 a.m. to 6 p.m. When was this day going to end? When was I going to see the sun and the mountains? The day was endless. I was yet to learn that the sun, during the winter, was only to be enjoyed at week-ends. Two years at Senghenydd and the shyness of the farm boy gave place to the chatty freedom of the Welsh colliery district.

1938

GOING SOUTH

Joe Thomas

I was twenty-one and newly married—so leaving Bethesda was not an easy matter. We'd surely miss the lovely country all around us—for we had Snowdon facing our front door. And then again—Bethesda was such a quiet place. Our only interests were work and chapel, and we could speak nothing but Welsh. To leave home seemed like a great adventure. My longest journey, so far, had been twenty-five miles, and at that distance from Bethesda I felt I was still at home. But Dowlais was two hundred miles away—that was different. It meant a new world, and because it was new we were timid. The only thing that helped us was to remember that Lizzie (*his sister*) was there. She—anyway—had not been swallowed alive by Dowlais. Perhaps we'd be all right, too.

And so, leaving my wife behind, I made the journey with my father. We arrived at Dowlais in the dark—at least it would have been dark in Bethesda. But here the sky was lit up with terrible flames. We crept out of our carriage not knowing what to expect, and stood on the platform staring at what we thought must be half the town on fire. Lizzie had come to meet us, and she tried her best to get my father to look at her. But *his* eyes were on those flames, and when at last he did notice her his first words were—not "How are you?"—but, "Lizzie fach, what terrible place is this?"

Next day we prepared for work in the pits, and then we had our second surprise. In Bethesda we went to work in white trousers—white smocks—and a collar and tie. The dust of the quarry was a clean dust, easily brushed off—it did more harm to our insides than to our clothes. We went to chapel on week-days in our working clothes, but in colliers' clothes, with no collar and tie, we felt undressed. I couldn't see how I looked, and I can only hope I didn't look as bad as my father.

In Bethesda I went up to my work, but in Bedlinog I had to go down, and that first drop was terrifying. It wouldn't be right to say that my heart was in my throat, because I didn't know where it was. I didn't even know where I was. All I remember is clutching my father and waiting for what I felt sure was going to be my last bump in the world. When it came, I was so surprised that I decided on the spot never to be afraid of anything I'd meet in Dowlais. We were on night-shift, and I spent most of my time in a daze, bumping against everything that couldn't move out of my way.

My father and I had to separate for work, but we arranged to meet at the top at the end of the shift. When I got up to the fresh air again, I searched for him everywhere—but there was no sign of him. It was a chilly morning, and seeing a fire I made for it. A collier, warming his hands, made room for me, but I was too shy to speak to him. We just stood there and nodded to each other—to show there was no ill feeling. Along came a man with a "Hoi, don't you want to catch the 'cwbs' to-day?" "Of

course I do," said I, and my companion at the fire jumped
with surprise. "Joe bach," said he, "is it you?" We had
never seen ourselves with black faces before, we had a
good laugh and I believe this helped us to forget the
shocks of the night before.

1938

THE QUARRYMAN

O. Madog Williams

A serious accident had taken place. In the deepest gallery
men were seen carrying a comrade to a waggon. As it
winded its way to the surface we could see the prostrate
form of a very popular work-mate. His hair was dyed red
with his own blood. He had a distant look and a mute
agony lodged in his eyes. He talked with his comrades as if
nothing had happened. Then his voice dropped into a low
tender strain, so musical, intense and sincere and full
of emotion as he sang a well known Welsh hymn, which
described the agony of Jesus on the cross. He seemed to
be painless and lost in the thought of another's pain. This
made a tremendous impression on me. It taught me that
Christianity was not, as I thought, a dry orthodox creed
and a life-sapping theology, but a vital and life-giving
power that enabled men to conquer and overcome their
difficulties.

The quarrymen, I knew, were a mixed group. Heroic,
fond of music, angling and poaching, poetry and literature.
In short, men of philosophical and reflective mind; of
abiding passion for knowledge who, in conjunction with
miners, out of their meagre earnings helped to build
Universities and were ready to sacrifice for others. Yes,
this valley in Snowdonia has a romantic association for
me, not because rugged grandeur and loveliness inter-
mingle there. I am fascinated with it because over every

inch of it hovers the spirit of Saints and unconquerable Warriors. Its grandeur for me is in its association with the modest, talented and noble-minded quarryman, who a generation ago, gave my country preachers like John Jones, Talysarn, Robert Jones, Llanllyfni, and Robert Roberts, Clynnog, and today not a few University professors and poets, around whose homes the future will weave legends and traditions. And this is not only true of Nantlle Vale, but of all the slate-quarry districts and of the coal-mining valleys of the South.

In most respects the quarryman of North Wales is not unlike his brother in the industrial South. The Welsh miner too is modest, talented and courageous. In spite of his poverty and adversity today, he never whines nor complains but reveals a spirit of fortitude which passeth understanding. When deprived of the necessaries of life he never displays his poverty. When cast down, he never shows his sores, he is too independent and dignified for that. Most of the South Wales miners are short, dark and sturdy, of Iberian stature, with dark brown eyes glittering with lively humour, and quick intelligence. Restless and active it seems as if their bodies were charged with dynamic power. The miner's strides are short and quick; the quarryman's long and leisurely. The miner's walk suggests alertness, a ready wit and business ability. The quarryman's walk seems to indicate thought, poetry and contemplation.

1938

FOUNDRYMAN

William Glynn-Jones

I see myself as a young lad again. On the threshold of life, at sixteen years of age. With shoulders hunched, head bowed, hands in tattered, liningless pockets I pass through the doors of the small, red-bricked time-office and stumble along between the curving rails that shimmer faintly in the reddened glow from the steel furnace. A wreath of grey smoke curls over the foundry roof. Wide tongues of flame shoot out from the gas producing plant to lick the base of the rain-smoked scrap dump beneath the yard crane.

I stoop through the needle's eye of the coreshop door, then, groping in the subdued light, slide open the door leading into the steel foundry. The place is silent, weird; another world of sleep, of things inanimate. Dim lights shine down, ranged along the high, soot-covered walls like a row of yellow buttons. The saddled roof is in darkness. Shadows fall across the dry, dusty floor. Mounds of brown, clayey moulding sand stretches along the centre of the foundry.

Shovels, their well worn handles sticking up like fence posts, their silvery blades embedded in the brown sand; tall iron rammers; rusty, dented buckets; moulding boxes red with rust or blackened with soot—they are all there to welcome me to the new day that has come.

In the dark corners near the mould-drying stoves and the water boshes, and beneath the furnace arch, grey, indistinct forms huddle together. These are my companions and fellow workers; moulders, improvers, apprentices, labourers, gantrymen—all clad in greasy dungarees, their faces hideous in the yellow light. Here they sit and gossip, taking advantage of the few minutes' grace before the foreman steps down from his office on the high platform at the top end of the foundry.

The seven o'clock hooter blows. The foreman's office

door opens, and all at once the grey figures startle into activity and disperse to the many untenanted moulds scattered along the foundry floor. From other corners men seep out of the shadows. Buckets of water are thrown over the dry banks. Shovels are grasped and the sand turned over and mixed. Labourers squat on their haunches, and with elbows resting on knees, riddle the damp mixture through inch-meshed sieves which they hold before them.

The gantrymen climb hand over hand up the iron ladders reaching to the steel cages, and crouch over their gears high above the arc lights.

The moulders clamber into the massive cast-iron boxes where the mould patterns are embedded. They spit into their hands. Ice-cold steel pneumatic rammers are gripped; wrists flick.

Suddenly the foundry is filled with thunder as the gantries roll along the girder tracks. The sharp, insistent "Ratatatat! Ratatatat!" of the pneumatic rammers bark in accompaniment. Then, the "bumper" jerks into life with a loud, deep-throated "Whoomp! Whoomp!" Its thumping and wheezing seem to shake the very walls, and the thick layer of soot which covers the window washes falls to the floor in a shower of black snow.

1947

SPEAKING FOR LABOUR

Charles Griffiths

The turning point in my life in Dowlais came with the great strike of the miners in 1898. For six months practically the whole of the coal-field was idle, and distress was acute. The miners had no great organisation which could provide strike pay, but married men obtained relief from the Board of Guardians, while single men had to fend for themselves. In return for this relief we had to do a certain amount of task-work—stone breaking in the various stone yards of Dowlais. We were paid at the end of each day, and every evening I drew a note for eightpence and fourpence in hard cash. This was the relief for my wife and myself.

There were hundreds of workmen in these stone yards, and advantage was taken of their discontent to spread the doctrines of the I.L.P. Willie Wright, an organiser of the movement, and Dai Davies, Pant, held meetings there regularly. There was always a rush to attend these meetings, and at the right moment these two brought the great Keir Hardie to the stone yards. The effect was tremendous. He spoke to them as a miner to miners—he told them to organise—and when the strike was over, there was a rush to join the Miners' Federation. This marked the real beginning of the Labour Movement in Dowlais and Merthyr. The fight is now over—the town has been won for Labour—but it was no easy fight. The old Liberal tradition among the workmen died hard. We were only about a dozen at the beginning, the task looked hopeless—but we had been fired by the enthusiasm of Keir Hardie, and were ready to do anything for him.

Our great problem was to get the men to listen to us—now that they were at work again. Some of our speakers were so enthusiastic that they preached hard facts, hard facts, and nothing but hard facts. The men weren't used to this. They liked a meeting after the 'Mabon' style—plenty of singing. Whenever Mabon got into a difficulty with a meeting, he always started them singing—and the difficulty vanished.

We started singing at our meetings, and in between the songs we told them some good home truths. To improve our public speaking we went regularly out into the country and practised our speeches on the sheep grazing peacefully on the mountain.

1938

RHONDDA 1874

David Williams

When we came to Cwmparc in 1874, the Rhondda was opening up and full of life. One after another the pits were being sunk. Houses were built in hundreds all along the valley and, of course, chapels were springing up in scores.

In those days work was so plentiful in the Rhondda that the people crowded into the valley before there was enough houses for them. Very often there would be eight or nine men lodging in one house and when four of them got up from bed to go to the early shift, the other four would be ready to get into their beds after coming in from the night shift. The beds were never empty. My butties and I used to spend our spare time in the nights learning music and we had to learn to read tonic solfa from the beginning. If one of us made a mistake, he got what we called a good "cob." That is, his hair pulled.

1938

SHARING

Thomas Jones

I once thought that I was settled for life in the Mynydd Colliery near Swansea. I was twenty-six, with a wife and four children, earning good money and having a house of my own and everything I wanted. Then, in 1896, things went wrong in the colliery and I was only allowed to work two days a week. Well, I couldn't keep a family on that and I dreaded poverty and hunger. Some of my friends used to come down for a weekend from the Rhondda. "What do you want to sit here for?" they said. "There's plenty of work to be had up there, mun." I decided to go and went up to Maerdy. My friends were right, there *was* plenty of work in the Rhondda. As soon as I went on top of the pit, I had a job straightaway to start the next day. Anybody could find a job in Maerdy in those days. They never turned anyone away. If a man had only one arm or one leg, they'd find some work for him in the colliery.

Of course, I was in lodgings at first. There was five of us in the same lodgings. There were beds in nearly every room and often we were sleeping in the beds during the night and the night men in the same beds during the day. Yes, you can imagine the scene, all of us arriving home and preparing for the tub. We were stripped to the waist and two of us washed the top part first. Then two other colliers would wash the top part in the same tub. We had to do that because the landlady was not very willing to boil too much water. And what fires there were in those days. We would think nothing of shoving a bucketful on the fire but now I carry the lumps of coal in my hand and see that nearly every cinder is burned out.

In the morning when dressing together to work, we'd find it difficult to put our hands on our own clothes. I have gone to work many a time wearing another lodger's stockings and boots of a different pair, but we were earning good money and, although we never saw daylight in the winter until Saturday, we were a jolly crowd and enjoying life in the good old Rhondda.

1938

84

RATS, BIRDS AND BARE KNUCKLES

Jack Jones

The strip of ground between the row and the brook was the playground for the children, was a drying and meeting place for the women, and a moping ground for the men when they lacked the means to raise the money for the pub. Then they would sit around the ashpit. Sometimes they would empty the ashpit to make a sort of cock-pit of it. They would put a live rat, the biggest they could get hold of and a veteran jackdaw that couldn't fly, down into the empty ashpit and then poke them with sticks to make them fight.

Sometimes the men themselves would fight each other, bare-knuckle and stripped to the waist. This was frowned upon by the people of the row for the recognised place for bare-knuckle fights, the *twmp*, was only a couple of hundred yards up the hill and there two men could fight it out without having their wives shrieking at them from their doorsteps . . .

There was only one water tap for our row and the houses behind and that was fixed to the wall at halfway point in the bottom row. On the recognised washing days the supply was often less than the demand and women would throughout the day be seen with buckets and pans waiting their turn to go to the tap which after having been heavily taxed in the earlier part of the day would only yield a trickle and fill one bucker per half-hour. Losing patience the women would go down to the brook, when there was enough water to cover the many dead cats and dogs, and fill their buckets there.

They had plenty of coal to boil the poison out of it, they said.

1964

MEN AGAINST OWNERS

Arthur Horner

Arthur Horner was General Secretary of the National Union of Mineworkers from 1946 until he retired in 1959. Before that he had been President of the South Wales Miners.

I was selling something—labour power and they had to buy it. I was selling a perishable commodity—it had to work or it had to die. And the coal-owners couldn't remain the coal-owners unless they bought what I had to sell. That's the real underlying purpose of 100% membership of the Union. It is to prevent the employers being able to buy in a market outside of your control. And labour power is as much a commodity as cabbages or potatoes and very much of a resemblance to it because of it isn't disposed of it will rot.

I never depended on their goodwill. I had no social relations with them at all. I never had anything to do with them outside the meetings and in the meetings themselves it was a very impersonal matter. And we depended on the outcome of the negotiations and that depended in its turn on the relative strengths. I never had any illusion that we'd get anything out of the owners because of kindness of heart—I know that we'd get what we were strong enough to take. Many people have been puzzled as to why strikes lessened in my time as compared to previous times. And it was because of that policy. Unless I saw a reasonable chance of winning a victory I would never sacrifice the men unnecessarily, because a strike means an awful lot to people who have to wait for a pay day.

I remember Sir Evan *(Williams, Chairman of the South Wales coal owners)* saying to me one day across the table when we were negotiating an Engineers Institute in Cardiff: "Can you tell me, Mr. Horner, why men get up at five o'clock in the morning, go to the top of the pit, through the rain, travel up a siding two or three miles and then they hear there's a pit-head meeting"—he was arguing to abolish pit-head meetings—"And some of them without knowing what the dispute was about walk back. Why do people do it?"

I remember telling him, "Well, I think I know. In every miner there is a subconscious fear that this is his day—the day when he might be killed or seriously injured. He never tells anybody about it—but he feels it, and if some thing happens even after he's taken all that trouble, that relieves him of that fear, he takes it. And that's why they come home sometimes—without rhyme or reason.

And I sympathise with that fear because you see in Wales men and women who are not very passionately in love—a man and his wife. There's one thing she always does, is see him off in the morning and kiss him good morning even though they don't do it any other time."

1962

STOWAWAY

Captain Tom James

As a boy most of my spare time after school hours was spent playing around the quays of the North Dock, and my sole ambition was to go to sea. I tried many times to get a job as a cabin boy or deck boy, in fact, anything that would take me to sea. But all in vain. Then I made up my mind to stow away. So one evening while playing around jib-boom corner, I noticed a brigantine all ready loaded for sea and waiting for the tide. She was called the *Ocean Queen* of Jersey.

As her crew was busy working at one end of the ship, I watched my chance and slipped aboard without being observed and hid myself down a kind of booby-hatch that led to her hold full of coal, and made myself as comfortable as possible. I must have slept right through the night, for when I awoke the ship was at sea, and the sun was pouring through the hatch scuttle. I waited a while before going on deck, and when I popped my head above the booby-hatch I was seen by one of the crew, who shouted out "Where the devil did you come from?". I told him that I was a stowaway. He took me at once to the captain who was looking through a pair of binoculars. When he saw me, he scowled and looked so fierce that I commenced to cry. He asked me a lot of questions as to how I got aboard and if any member of the crew had assisted me.

After I had answered all his questions, he turned to look at the land that was not far away. Then he said to me, "Do you see the island over there? Well, it's full of savages, and I'm going to land you there. It's called Lundy Island." I believed him and begged him not to land me there. Whereupon he smiled, and told the sailor to take me to the galley and to see that I had a good feed and a wash, for I was as black as a sweep from sleeping on the coal all night. After that the Captain and crew treated me very kindly.

1938

SHANGHAIED

CAPTAIN TOM JONES

In May, 1889, I was paid off at Boston, Massachusetts, and stayed in a boarding-house waiting for a ship to take me home. But I was shanghaied instead.

One evening, as I was just going out for a stroll, the boarding-house mistress called after me, "Tom Jones, come back here and breast the bar." This meant a free drink on the house. I went back, had a few swigs of raw rye whiskey . . . and remembered no more. When I came to myself I was lying in a heap aboard a stern-wheeler, for I could hear its paddle thrashing the water.

I crept along and suddenly I heard the strains of music which seemed to come from behind the closed cabin door. I pushed the door ajar, but was prevented from entering by a rough man who forbade me to enter and offered me a glass of whiskey. Before very long I became unconscious again.

The second time I came around I was amazed to find myself aboard a small steam launch in the Bay at Portland, Maine, in company with half a dozen doped sailors. It was pitch dark and soon we sheered alongside a huge barque —the "Venezuela" belonging to Yarmouth, Nova Scotia— and loaded to her masthead with timber. We were dragged half-dazed aboard and thrust down a gaping hole in the deck. As I lay there gasping and wondering what to do, a booming, coarse voice shouted down to us, "Come along there, you lime-juicers, come along." As I clambered up, a bully of a Second Mate clouted me unmercifully about the head. He mustered us all on deck, and the mate talked to us and we all decided to stay aboard.

Next day, we proceeded on our passage to Buenos Aires. All the way down the Second Mate led us a dog's life. But we had our revenge upon him. Just before we entered Buenos Aires a crowd of us were manning the capstan when I accidentally trod on the heel of a Swedish sailor. At once he turned round on me and, in an angry voice, challenged me to fight. Whereupon the bullying second mate came up on us and said that if there was any fighting to be done aboard his ship, he would be the one to do it. Suddenly a big Irishman, who for a long time had it in for the bully, pulled out a capstan bar and floored him. We all seized the unconscious Mate and dragged him aft, and left him lying before the cabin door. He ceased to bully us after that.

When the ship arrived in port, all the crew except me and the bullying second mate cleared out. I made the passage back to St. John's in her, and later got a ship home to Liverpool, after being away from home for over three years.

1938

SUMMER DAY IN THE DOCKS

T. E. THAIN

At the end of Tyndall Street was the wall of the Bute Top Yard. In this yard were repaired the locomotives that did the hauling and shunting around the docks of such goods as weren't handed direct by the railway locos. As the Taff Vale Railway embankment came up against the yard the retaining wall of the embankment formed an arm which cut off the pavement outside. This in its very nature became the sitting out place for the workers, in the warm weather, during the breakfast and dinner hour. When I got a bit older I sat out there myself.

From this vantage point all the events of Tyndall Street could be observed. The number of people who went into the Red Lion, the movements of the gentry of the street and on special occasions one might have the satisfaction of seeing Father O'Sullivan helping one of his obstreperous congregation home with a stick. But that was a rare treat, since the very threat of "His Reverence" was enough to send the most rebellious flying for shelter. It was seated on this pavement that Ianto Evans persuaded us to join in a gamble on Victor Wild, who came home at 25 to 1 with the result that most of the street bookies were missing on settling day, the whole of Cardiff Docks having decided to back the same horse.

One beautiful warm summer day in the dinner hour we were sitting with our backs to the wall and contemplating the heat waves from the wall of the Red Lion, the experts smoking shag and the young men, unseasoned apprentices,

Cinderella cigarettes, when a woman dashed out of one of the houses on the other side of the road followed closely by a gent brandishing a poker with which he obviously intended to give her a lesson. He caught the poor woman in the middle of the street and knocked her down with a shrewd blow and proceeded to carry on with the good work. A man who was passing stepped into the road and seized him by the arm. Alas for our would-be hero, the villain turned on him and slashed at him with the poker and the hero retreated from what was possibly his first effort in lifesaving. The ruffian then returned to his victim. However, a coaltrimmer was proceeding to work carrying over his shoulder the big shovel with which he guided the coal in the bowels of the ships. The noble fellow grasped the situation in one glance. He stepped off the pavement, lifted the shovel high in the air and brought it down with a crash on the head of the villain collapsed unconscious on the body of the woman. The coaltrimmer replaced his shovel on his shoulder and proceeded on his way, with the air of a man who knows a deed well done.

1949

CHARITY?

HARRY GREEN

Less than a month ago, I picked up from a secondhand book stall a pamphlet issued by the Neath Board of Guardians in 1875. It was the annual list of Neath paupers, those unfortunates who had been 'in receipt of' outdoor relief. Among them were the names of my paternal great-grandfather, my great-grandmother, and four of their children. There it was recorded for the eyes of ratepayers anxious to know where their money was going, that my great-grandfather and his family received an allowance of one shilling and sixpence a week, sixpence more than was needed to buy a shroud.

I flushed as I looked on that record, but not for shame, not for family shame. My great-grandfather's life was known to me as the life of a proud, hard-working man. He was an Englishman, and lost his first man's job on a farm because he voted against the squire's nominee in an open election. He became a railway construction navvy, and I am proud to record that he was one of that gang of navvies who built the Vale of Neath railway. I flushed because that name in the list of paupers brought every other name to life; I saw the aged and sick of a small Welsh town in the last decade of the nineteenth century, holding out reluctant hands to the hard-faced Guardians of the Poor, the drapers, the mill-owners, the squires, the men they had sweated for all the days of their lives. I saw a host of labourers dedicated to a life of toil with nothing at the end of it but the bitterness of the Poor Law's grudging pittance. I saw children too, who must look for life not to the fathers who loved them but to the Guardians' officer who would balance their lives in a ledger and publish their names as a burden on the ratepayers.

And yet, for all that, my great-grandfather and his family were lucky. Does that sound strange? Can a man be called "lucky" who has lost his livelihood and must depend on official charity—than which there is nothing colder—to keep him from starvation? He can. My great-grandfather was spared the last crowning misery which he and his family might have suffered from the hands of the benevolent State. He was granted *outdoor* relief. He wasn't forced to enter the doors of the Union Workhouse, to be parted from his wife and children. Had his misfortunes come but thirty years earlier, they would have struck a great deal harder. We know these things. We have read them in our history books; but no history book ever written drives home the edged truth like a personal document written about a place that is known to you.

92   *1947*

GAZOOKA

GWYN THOMAS

An extract from a radio feature

By the beginning of June 1926 the hills were bulging with a clearer loveliness than they had ever had before. No smoke rose from the great chimneys to write messages on the sky that saddened and puzzled the minds of the young. The endless journeys of coal-trams on the inclines, loaded on the upward run and empty on the down, ceased to rattle through the night and mark our dreams. The parade of nailed boots on the pavements at dawn fell silent, and day after glorious day came up over hills that had been restored by a quirk of social conflict to the calm they lost a hundred years before. When the school holidays came we took to the mountain tops, joining the liberated pit ponies among the ferns on the broad plateaus. That was the picture for us who were young. For our fathers and mothers, there was the inclosing fence of hinted fearts, fear of hunger, fear of defeat. And then, out of the quietness and the golden light, partly to ease their fret, a new excitement was born. The carnivals and the jazz bands.

Rapture can sprout in the oddest places and it certainly sprouted then and there. We formed bands by the dozen, great lumps of beauty and precision, a hundred men and more in each, blowing out their songs as they marched up and down the valleys, amazing and deafening us all. Their instruments were gazookas, with an occasional drum. Gazookas; small tin zeppelins through which you hummed the tune as loudly as possible. Each band was done up in the uniform of some remote character never before seen in Meadow Prospect; Foreign Legionnaires, Chinamen, Carabinieri, Grenadiers, Gauchos, or what we thought these performers looked like. There was even one group of lads living up on the cold slopes of Mynydd

Coch who did themselves up as Eskimos, but they were liquidated because even Matthew Sewell the Sotto, our leading maestro and musical adviser, couldn't think up a suitable theme song for boys dressed as delegates from the Arctic.

And with the bands came the fierce disputes inseparable from any attempt to promote a little beauty on this planet, the too-hasty crowding of chilled men around its small precious flame. The thinkers of Meadow Prospect, a small and anxious fringe, gathered in the Discussion Group at the Library and Institute to consider this new marvel. I can see the room now and hear their voices. Gomer Gough, the chairman, broad, wise, enduring and tolerant as our own scarred hillsides, sitting at his table beneath two pictures, a photograph of Keir Hardie and an impression, done in charcoal and a brooding spirit, of the betrayal and death of Llewelyn the Last. Then there was my uncle, Edwin Pugh, called Pugh the Pang for his way of wincing at every mention of the bruises sustained by our species in the cause of being so special.

1953

A DEADLY EVIL

S. O. DAVIES

Surely it is not necessary for me to tell you that we M.P.s for Wales regard unemployment as one of the most deadly evils. In fact, there is to us only one greater evil, and that is war. Unemployment was the evil that drove nearly half-a-million of our people from Wales between the two wars. It is the evil that breaks up our homes and our Welsh communities, and destroys our culture and our sense of nationhood.

1949

PRESERVING SELF-RESPECT

ELFAN REES

When a man loses his work, it's not only his wages that he loses. There are a number of other vital things to take into account. He misses the opportunity for expressing himself which work normally gives him; he loses the fellowship of his workmates; he misses the sense of membership of an active community; and worst of all, he tends to lose his self-respect.

Now, as I see it, society has a double responsibility towards the unemployed man. First, it has to provide some alternative to his wages; and secondly, it has to help him in his own efforts to preserve his real self. The community carries out its first duty through unemployment insurance benefit and Unemployment Assistance.

There are, of course, at least two opinions as to the adequacy of these payments and the way they are determined. The second duty, the task of helping the unemployed to preserve their individuality as self-respecting men and women, has, so far, not been carried out by the estate.

1938

AN END TO EXPERIMENT

DR. BRINLEY THOMAS

The voluntary Social Service Movement is a commendable attempt to get the unemployed to get more out of life. It cannot within its limits do anything substantial to increase their purchasing power and material standard of living. We recognise that the practice of allowing voluntary agencies full scope to experiment before the State intervenes with a nationally financed scheme is an old British custom. That's how it was with Poor Relief and primary education. But such a practice can also be a convenient smoke-screen for the lack of State policy.

I feel that ten years of dire poverty in South Wales is a sufficiently long experimental period. The material standard of living of the people over forty-five, thrown out of the economic system for good, and destined to live in South Wales for the rest of their lives, is a national responsibility. This is not a matter for voluntary experiments. It involves legislation reforming our system of pensions, social insurance, and possibly introducing family allowances.

It may mean unconventional measures. British democracy has yet to show itself equal to the difficult problems of long-term unemployment which called the voluntary Social Service movement into being.

1938

EXPORTING THE WELSH GENIUS

LADY RHYS WILLIAMS

There is no need for Welsh people to feel beholden to the British taxpayer for the contributions now received towards the cost of dole payments, and of health and education services, since even ten years of distress and financial dependency upon Britain cannot yet have balanced the high figures of taxation contributed by Wales to the National Exchequer, during the many prosperous years which preceded the slump, and especially during the War. In any case, the 300,000 young Welsh workers, educated and cared for at the expense of Wales, who are now serving English interests, and the benefit of whose productive years will accrue to the British Exchequer, represent, I think, a generous enough return for any financial assistance received by Wales today.

Granted that these contributions are no more than our

right, are indeed less than Welsh standards of generosity would provide if the position were reversed, yet it seems obvious that the lot of the unemployed areas of Wales would be infinitely worse if these payments were no longer forthcoming out of English pockets. It may be true that good government is no substitute for self-government, but self-government is, alas, small compensation for an empty larder.

The case of Wales must be heard, and her wrongs must be redressed. I have always felt that we sorely lack an advocate in the councils of the British Cabinet, and the appointment of a Secretary for Wales is, I think, long overdue.

I have grieved over the loss which Wales is daily suffering by the constant emigration of her finest citizens. There is no doubt that this is the cruellest of all the many sorrows which she has been called upon to suffer in recent years. Materially and humanly speaking it is disastrous, but spiritually it may be the greatest of all her gifts to the cause of human welfare.

For these thousands of young souls are carrying the Welsh genius for loyalty, the Welsh sense of individual liberty, of family devotion, of community spirit, of patriotic fervour, and yet of international sympathy and understanding, out into the world which needs these qualities so badly today.

1937

HARD FACTS AND COLD REASON

Hilary Marquand

The writer, later Labour M.P. for East Cardiff, was Director of Industrial Surveys of South Wales in 1931 and 1936.

About 100,000 or more workers from South Wales have found employment in new industries during the last fourteen or fifteen years. But they have found it in England. Every day, as you all know, young men and women and boys and girls, are going off to new jobs in England. It is very difficult indeed to calculate the rate at which such migration reduces the labour supply. But we have made a shot at it; and we came to the conclusion that if migration continues, then by 1943, without the introduction of any large new industries, the present surplus of labour will have disappeared. But though we all want the surplus to be absorbed, do we want it to be absorbed in this way—by finding work in England? *We* say *"No."* But we do not say it for sentimental reasons, however important these may be. We have stuck to hard facts and cold reason, and on economic grounds alone we believe we have established beyond contradiction that new industries can and should be established in South Wales . . .

. . . But if new industries are to be introduced, we must do all we can to make them successful. Therefore, the latter part of the Survey Report is concerned with suggestions for the improvement of facilities. Most important is transport. We have considered very carefully all the pros and cons of the proposal to build a new road bridge over the Severn. And we definitely conclude that such a bridge ought to be built, not merely to encourage the tourist trade, but as an essential requirement of new light industries. If the bridge is built, it must be served with new approach roads, and we suggest that the road along the north of the coalfield from Abergavenny to Merthyr be improved and extended to link up the distressed towns at the tops of the valleys with the new bridge and with Carmarthen and West Wales.

This should provide much needed work for the unemployed of these towns, and would relieve the pressure on the congested main road through Cardiff, Bridgend, Port Talbot and Swansea.

1937

DISILLUSION AND CHANGE

Dr. Brinley Thomas

That the pulse of community life should be beating as strongly as it is in many a struggling district is a tribute to that courageous spirit which deserves to triumph over the most adverse circumstances. The character of the people has been sorely tried—one is reminded of the drama of the Book of Job—and in spite of it all there is an indomitable will to preserve the fabric of society.

This does not mean that the younger generation agree with the outlook of their fathers. A mental readjustment has been going on. It would have been a matter for surprise if a wave of scepticism had not swept over the young people. Their illusions have disappeared one after another in the hard school of distress. Things which their fathers and their grandfathers regarded as fairly firm and permanent have proved to be short-lived. South Wales is much more closely connected with the rest of the Kingdom than it was ever before. The valleys are no longer closed communities. Is it any wonder that the boys of South Wales, when they leave school to-day, are not at all keen to go down the pits? I think it is interesting, by the way, to recall that in the Agreement signed between the South Wales Miners' Federation and the Coal Owners in 1937 the rates of wages for boys employed underground were increased, in the case of the older boys by about 1/6

($7\frac{1}{2}p$) a shift; and for the first time a schedule of minimum rates was arrived at for boys working on the surface.

This seems to show an awareness on the part of the coal owners that, even though the industry has shrunk so much, there may yet be a shortage of juvenile labour. The Reports of the Juvenile Advisory Committees have often reported that boys now ask for any employment "except underground." This is a remarkable example of a re-adjustment in outlook, when we remember that before the depression it used to be regarded as the natural and almost preordained thing for boys on leaving school to go down the mine . . .

. . . Though the outlook is none too cheerful we would do well to keep a sense of perspective. If the general trend is in the direction of a falling population, and if this will be a richer community, there may be some grounds for hope. At the present time the strongholds of the Welsh language are the agricultural districts. It is not losing ground there as fast as it is in the industrial areas. I am not forgetting the quarry districts of North Wales. As far as the North is concerned, it may well be that its economic foundations will come to rely more on tourist traffic. If so, it will be up to the North Walian to see to it that the Welsh flame does not become dimmer owing to the necessity for attracting English visitors. If Welsh agriculture could support more people than it is now doing, there would be a better chance for the survival of Welsh.

The prospect seems to be that the number of people living in Wales will decline, and the proportion of this smaller population which will care for Welsh culture will not be very large. If the policy of transference is wound up and if the economic foundations of Wales are strengthened through the creation of new industries, the decline needn't be as great. Nevertheless, if the amount of wealth per head will be double what it is to-day, the economic obstacle which is powerful to-day will lose some of its strength.

As we gradually overcome the economic problem we are enabled to turn more and more of our energies to the things of the mind and the spirit. If the economic possibilities for the people of Wales in fifty years can be regarded optimistically, then, though the population may fall to a million or less, the interest in Welsh culture may be *relatively* greater than it is to-day. As for those who have migrated to England, some of them will maintain their national characteristics, many will flock back to Wales if they get half a chance, and perhaps the majority will be assimilated into the English community. All this is pure speculation. But one of the lessons of this whole series of talks is that we must accustom ourselves to a shrinking community. This era of rapidly expanding population was just a temporary phase in history. To-day we are able to foresee to some extent the future course of the population. There is ample time in which to make the necessary adjustments if we apply our minds to the problems now.

1938

BITTER IDLENESS

B. L. COOMBES

We've had a lean time in the mining areas until lately, but I do not see much signs of this in the younger generation as far as their bodily development is concerned, for physically most of them seem to be superior to the older folk. But it is in their mental attitude and the way they react to the working conditions that one can trace the effect of the long years of depression. In those days that boys from the smaller mining towns were fortunate because they lived close to the pits and usually got what work was going.

Taken on the whole, these boys are quieter and easier to control. The boys from the larger towns are not so amenable and appear to have little respect for the advice of older and more experienced workmen. The institutions of the mining communities—such as the Miners' Federation, welfare halls and parks and the places of worship have little value in their sight. Middle-aged men know well that long years of intense struggle were needed before these institutions were founded and developed; they know what mining life was like before they came into being.

It seems to me that the years in which these lads saw their fathers and brothers idling about the street corners, or watching each hopeless day recede before the misery of the next, has left an imprint on their minds which will be very difficult to erase. You cannot allow a whole community to remain idle without leaving a bitterness in the thoughts of the people who are concerned.

Yet most of these lads have some excellent qualities. They are loyal to one another and are usually very good natured. When at work they work hard, very hard, and they show an eagerness to learn—if the right kind of teacher is available. I want to stress that point about teachers. These lads distrust, and usually with very good reason, anything that has any suggestion of officialdom. To them it seems that the old political parties and the religious bodies have failed them completely and now they are waiting for something new that they can trust.

1943

WOMEN IN ADVERSITY

Jack Jones

During the twenty-six years I worked underground, I witnessed hundreds of incidents which were revelations of the remarkable courage of the men of the mines. I could talk for hours of men who willingly risked their lives in attempts to save others. Falls of roof, flooding, explosions . . . men volunteering for almost certain death for the sake of an injured and trapped pal. "Hopeless or not, I'm having a go . . ." The trapped men themselves singing Welsh hymns during the days and nights of anxious waiting, without food or drink, but still singing, their undying spirit challenging and defying oncoming death.

Then the women of our Welsh mining communities, the mothers, wives and sweethearts of the miners who have responded to their country's call now as well as they did from 1914 to 1918. Why bring in the women? Well, for this reason. I have, more than once, been moved to tears when visiting the scene of a mining disaster. I've seen a South Wales mining township stricken to the heart by an explosion which, in the twinkling of an eye, robbed the place of the lives of 450 men and boys. *Then* the regal courage of the women of our mining communities shines like a beacon light through the gathering darkness of despair. Dozens of times the women-folk of the Welsh miners have had to face up to such blows, the heaviest of which have practically wiped out the working populations of little townships.

In addition to the major mining disasters of my time, these women have faced the daily fatalities and injuries in a way that compels unceasing admiration. Last, but not least, they saved the souls of their families alive through the years of the depression in the mining industry.

1941

LEAVING THE LAND

EDWARD NEVIN

In almost all developing countries agriculture has declined relatively to other industries, partly because as they get better off people spend a smaller part of their income on food, and partly because of the steady improvement of agricultural methods. But the fall in the rural population of Wales is more serious than, for example, in England. Firstly, a much bigger share of the Welsh rural population has been lost; secondly, the drift from the countryside has generally stopped in England, whereas it's still going on in Wales.

Why is there this drift from the Welsh countryside? The reasons are fairly familiar. So far as his work is concerned, the chap employed on a farm has been at a hopeless disadvantage compared with a similar man working in industry. His wages are lower; he works a longer day; if he has a cottage its rent is sometimes high and its condition almost invariably poor; he is out at all hours and in all weathers. And for the great majority the prospects of advancement towards the top of the ladder are pretty dim. The middle-aged miner or steel-worker may smile a bit at this; but to a school-leaver at the beginning of his working life it's rather important that a job should look as if it has a future. Illusion perhaps, but life often runs on illusions.

The country wives have their worries, too. Housing all too often in disrepair, sewerage and piped water luxuries unknown outside the larger towns, electricity and gas the same, the nearest neighbour miles away perhaps, a three or four mile trip on not-very-frequent buses for shopping, or a cinema, or a doctor's surgery; the same twice a day for the children to get to school.

Now the danger about a drift away from rural areas is that a vicious circle can be set up. If the lack of general amenities causes migration, the migration itself makes it more and more difficult to provide these amenities. Their cost increases if population becomes more thinly spread, simply because there are so many more miles of pipe or road or wire for each consumer. At the same time, the local authorities responsible for so many of these things are made poorer by the fall in the number and prosperity of their ratepayers. In 1951 a penny rate brought in less than £700 in Cardigan or Merioneth; in Glamorgan it brought in more than £11,000. So you have the circle—poor amenities drive out population, a falling population makes the provision of amenities more and more difficult, leading to further migration, and so on.

1954

BACK TO THE LAND

B. L. COOMBES

Until I was seventeen I lived on a small farm in Herefordshire. Now after a lapse of years, I am again back on the land—this time as tenant of a hill farm overlooking the Vale of Neath. I can imagine no greater contrast in farming conditions, for in Herefordshire the land was rich and easily worked because of its flatness, whilst here, in Wales, the wealth of the ground is below the surface in the coal seams and the surface is stony and poor. In Herefordshire, as I remember it, production was easy; but marketing—especially for the smaller grower—was difficult. With us here it is production which brings the worry, marketing is not the least trouble for everything is bought at our doors—and taken very gladly too—for the mining villages in the valley below.

We have been here three years and my fifty acres has been farmed in our spare time for I work by night in the colliery. You see, I work during the night underneath the land which I cultivate by day, and week-ends, and any spare time which I can discover. It's not setting yourself an easy task to tackle a double job like this (under difficult conditions) but we've made a go of it. My eighteen-year-old son helps me after *his* pit work and my wife gives all her time and interest to it. That's the most important thing with the family farm—having a wife who likes the life and the animals . . .

. . . Below, in these valleys the folk live in crowded villages over which the dust from the pit screens falls like dry rain. It drifts into the houses and lodges in the lungs of the people who live in them. The miners inhale this dust at their work, then come home to linger in an atmosphere which is nearly as bad.

Yet, all around them, sloping gently up from the valleys are immense stretches of hill land which have once been cultivated but are now idle and deserted. Walking across these slopes, you can see gardening memorials to the folly of the past—piles of stone where once there stood some prosperous farmstead and what's more, you don't need to travel far to pass a dozen of these ruins. But up there we have clean mountain air, unlimited land, plenty of clear water, stone without limit for the making of roads and buildings and electric power within very easy reach.

Also, and I know this because I work with them, there are scores of men here with an agricultural background or with a longing to work a small piece of land on their own and in the mind of every worker in these areas there is an ever present fear—the dread that pit dust will cripple his chest and shorten his life.

Is there a way in which we can relate these things for the benefit of the folk concerned? I think the part-time holding would help in many cases and I am not preaching without practice.

I want those families who have farming experience to get a part-time holding on the hill sides. Not large holdings, as that would mean too much work for them to handle. I think twelve acres would be ample—remember I am thinking of poorish land on a gentle slope. The beginning of it all would be a good road and with the material so near at hand this should not be a great difficulty. A slight spiral effect in construction will easily surmount most of the slopes here and the holdings could be built on a terraced plan with the higher ground left for mountain sheep.

Why couldn't the Forestry Commission plant avenues of trees along roads and also good windbreaks between each holding? A rustic seat every fifty yeards would be a boon also and then perhaps the valley folk would come up to see what was going on—to their very great benefit in both health and knowledge. The electric cables could be trenched alongside this road. If no reservoir was near, small ones could be made by damming the mountain streams—there are plenty of them everywhere. Anyway, a good supply of water and electricity must be available for the new houses that would have to be built; stone for their construction and that of the modern buildings for sheltering the stock could be quarried from the higher ground.

I want the women on these holdings to have all the comforts a town house gives . . . electric lighting and radio sets, electric irons and cleaners and so on; also there must be indoor taps and baths with hot water. Why should the hardest worked housewives have the least conveniences?

1943

WAR

Idris Davies

In 1914 I was nine years old, and on one July afternoon of
that year I sat in one of the classrooms of an elementary
school in my home town in South Wales, a small mining
town in Monmouthshire. The teacher was a rather
elderly spinster, slim, sharp featured, and slightly grey-
haired. I believe it was on the eve of the summer holiday,
and she was telling us about a big war that was starting far
away, beyond the sea. Germany and Austria were going
to fight Russia and France. It was all very fascinating to
me. Somehow or other Austria was glamorous. I could
see the soldiers of Austria marching in the sunshine, all
dressed in brilliant crimson and gold. Our teacher said
that such a war would be terrible. But I did not agree. I
could see the soldiers of Austria marching, and it would
be a pity to stop them. Her rather shrill voice was not in
tune to the music of my imagination, and I went home
quite pleased and excited, knowing that there would be a
great war as well as a long holiday.

The next thing I remember is the annual church tea-
fight held a few days afterwards on Bank Holiday Monday.
After the walking and the tea-drinking, all the people
went up to the vicarage field for the sports and the
fireworks. The field was just across the river, and behind
it were the black tips and the remains of a disused colliery.
It was an evening of brilliant sunshine. All the women
were in coloured dresses, and each woman wore an
immense hat, full of flowers. I remember my mother had
such a hat, and I thought it must be very heavy for her to
carry about. But there she was, in her big flowery hat,
talking to other women, in their big flowery hats, and
standing in the middle of the vicarage field. The brass
band was playing a few yards away, and big girls in white
and pink dresses were dancing in a ring; probably they

were girls of seventeen and eighteen, perhaps younger, but I thought they were very big and very beautiful.

I could hear my mother and her friends talking about the war. It was going to be terrible. Germany was so strong and mighty. The very sound of the word haunted me for some time. Germany, Germany . . . It seemed as if the word itself was filling the sky and stretching out in great letters across the river to the streets and the hills on the other side. I don't remember how the sports ended that day, nor seeing the fire-works later in the evening. But I was very impressed by the might of Germany. I could hear the women all the time telling one another: "Germany is so powerful, you know."

A few days afterwards I saw the local Territorials march through the streets to the railway station. They started from the Drill Hall, a very prosaic building down by the river. The Drill Hall is still there, and when I pass it, I always recall that summer morning in August 1914. A crowd of children had gathered outside, and we were watching the soldiers very intently. When they began marching, we started singing and shouting, and we followed the men in khaki throught he streets. It was great fun I thought, as I banged away at the empty tin in my hand. But I always remember one incident of that summer morning. As we marched along I saw an old woman on one of the doorsteps weeping, and she was surrounded by a group of young women. She had three sons in khaki, and they were marching past the door. Perhaps I was rather puzzled at seeing her weeping, but I know that whenever I passed that door afterwards I looked to see if she was there.

1940

MINERS AT WAR

ARTHUR HORNER

The mass of the miners are very highly patriotic; they love their country and desire to make it a better place to live in. The miners hate all forms of suppression, whether of free speech, free Press, or free people. They have always fought for free speech, free Press and for the right of a free people to exist in our own country. They love freedom and because fascism, nazi-ism, call it what you will, is the antithesis of all that is representative of freedom, they are convinced and loyal fighters in the struggle against these dark Forces. This is the reason why the mineworkers organisations have recorded their wholehearted support of the National War Effort expressed in the struggle of the United Nations. This is why the mineworkers everywhere can be depended upon to make the maximum contributions to the successful carrying through of that war effort until victory is achieved.

There are few illusions in the minds of the mineworkers based upon the possibility of future recognition and reward. They remember the lavish promises during the last war, and the terrible experiences which were forced upon them in the years following the war. The miners, however, realise that the period of depression, distress and misery in which we lived for many years would not compare with the hell which life would become if the Axis powers should win this war. Everything which is dear to the hearts of the mineworkers, would be destroyed in the orgy of bestiality which would be imposed upon us were this country defeated in the war.

1942

A NEGATION OF HUMANITY

JACK JONES

We went up a hill where there was trenches full of
Germans. We took the trenches and from there we went
up to Ypres, and there the slaughter was intensified. We
lost practically all our regiment. We stayed until we were
reinforced by drafts from home and we lost that lot.

Then I was burying people and helping wounded
people out, seeing chaps coming out with arms off and,
well, things too horrible to describe now. Yet in these
days they call that conventional warfare as though it was
something done in a flaming drawing-room.

I did fight to the best of my ability for the thirteen weeks
that I was in that great slaughter that wiped out a generation but the medals I got for it I am not very proud of.
War is a stupid business, conventional or nuclear or
whatever they like to call it, it is a negation of humanity.

1964

THE WELSH SOLDIER

TASKER WATKINS V.C. (LORD JUSTICE WATKINS)

When a Welshman goes to war he takes with him not only
his proud fighting spirit and his hymns and songs but he
takes also his acute and valuable sense of humour. This in
peace has brought him without much bitterness through
times of adversity and there have been plenty of those. It
is a humour which comes as quick as a flash, turns light on
the gloom and helps to ease the numbing pain of fear
which all men feel upon the start line of a battle.

It takes away the name a man was born with and gives
him something ridiculous but affectionate in its place. So
we had, among a host of others, Dai Q.M., and Sospan

Jones from Llanelli. Alas, brave Sospan the Pioneer Officer who will never see Llanelli again.

In the close fighting and slit trenches of Normandy this humour nourished the spirits of us all. Who amongst those of the 5th Welch who came back from there will ever forget Hill 112 Esquay, Evrecy-le-Grainville, Le Bon Repos, Fresney-le-Vieux and Bafour. A good memory is a fine thing but for those who were there it should not be too good. It should be good enough, however, to recall the great comradeship we enjoyed and which we shall never experience again.

1955

REPORTING THE WAR

WYNFORD VAUGHAN-THOMAS

For broadcasters like Wynford Vaughan-Thomas one of the greatest problems that faced them as war correspondents was the sheer size and weight of the recording equipment they had to use. It was some time before they could report from the front line.

We tried it at first with an anti-E-boat patrol but, of course, as soon as we got into action the thing was smashed up. I did one from a submarine off Bergen fjord, but we were depth-charged and that killed that one.

Then the Lancaster bomber came in and it had space in which you could take an engineer, all his gear and me up for'ard doing a recording. So it was, in a way, the first recording from actually in battle that we were able to make.

I can remember it very vividly. You came into a bullring of light. You felt like shrimps moving through luminous seaweed, dangerous seaweed, because once the searchlight gripped you, up came the flak and down you went.

Well, we dropped the bomb and, as we were dropping it, the voice of the rear-gunner in slow East Anglia drawl said: "Night-fighter attacking, sir." My insides sank and then we shot him down and we got out safely. Luck of the old Nick, we'd just dropped the big bomb and all these tracers went under us as we lifted.

After taking part in the Anzio landings, Wynford Vaughan-Thomas went on with the army to the South of France.

It was the most wonderful piece of war ever for me. We landed on my birthday, August 15th, in warm water in St. Tropez. A tremendous barrage went round and we rushed forward expecting to be mown down by German machine guns but, as we discovered afterwards, the Germans had pulled out the night before. And there advanced through the smoke an immaculately dressed Frenchman carrying a tray of iced champagne glasses.

We all stopped and he said: "Bienvenue, Monsieur, welcome, welcome. May I venture a little criticism? You are four years late."

Oh, what a campaign—it was known after in the troops as the champagne campaign although we were liberating Chateauneauf du Pape and Tavel and Burgundy.

1983

A CATHEDRAL BOMBED

R. T. WHITE

Within a few minutes of the warning, the sky over Llandaff was ablaze with incendiary bombs. I never saw anything more beautiful. My wife and I stood and watched it for a few minutes. It was like a gigantic firework display. Having seen my wife safely to a shelter, I made my way down to the Cathedral. One incendiary bomb dropped about a yard outside the Lady Chapel. I smothered it with a sandbag; then I went into the Cathedral, where the Dean met me. I went along the south aisle, leaving the Dean by the entrance door.

I had only gone about a dozen yards when there was a tremendous bang and a loud crash. I felt a terrific blow on my head, and the next thing I remember is lying under the wreckage unable to move. I was buried beneath the timbers and the stonework of the roof. I tried to shout for help, but I could only make a moaning noise. After what seemed an age, eight or nine men arrived, cleared away the debris, and carried me out of the Cathedral.

I remember no more until the following Sunday, when I saw the Bishop come into the hospital ward where I was lying. I believe the sight of the Bishop, and hearing his voice, started me on the way to recovery.

It was two months before I saw the Cathedral again. The damage was heart-breaking. Three parts of the roof was blown down, all the windows broken; the organ, which only eighteen months previously had been restored, was totally destroyed. The fine choir stalls were a mass of broken wood. The whole outlook was beyond description, and in my weak state it was more than I could bear.

1953

COUNTING THE COST

AILEEN DAVID

I have worshiped at Llandaff Cathedral all my life—in fact, I was baptised there eighty-two years ago—and in my time I have known five Bishops and eight Deans. So the dreadful results of the blitz was a great shock to me. I had the first shock when I came to Green. There, of course, many of the houses were badly blitzed, the tiles off the roofs and no glass in any of the windows. The whole of the Llandaff Green itself was covered with stones, tiles, broken masonry, broken glass, dust.

I picked my way carefully across, towards the lych gate, and it wasn't till I noticed a piece of tombstone with "In memory of" carved on it that it dawned upon me that much of this rubble must be pieces of our Cathedral.

As I went down the hill to see, the look of the ruin was much worse. There was a great hole in the roof and the doors had been broken in, and all the lovely early English windows on the south side, which in the fourteenth century had replaced the original Norman windows, were destroyed. I think it was then that I remembered that the pre-Raphaelite stained glass had been taken down and put in safety, as well as Rossetti's triptych and the little statue of the Madonna and Child from the Lady Chapel. But as I went in it looked a terrible ruin. Everything, pews, stalls, piled in heaps or lying flat—or else the stalls seemed to be hanging in the air. The altar itself was standing intact, which was a wonderful thing. The pulpit and the font, which also were pre-Raphaelite work, looked as usual, though later they had to be scrapped.

The light brass screen with its little coloured stones and lanterns, which I had loved since I was a child, hung twisted beyond repair. I met Mr. Guy Clarke, father of Mr. William Clarke, who loved the Cathedral and knew every stone of it, and we stood looking at it together. "This will cost at least £50,000," he said, but it was found

115

to be even more damaged than at first appeared. For at that first sight of it, I felt that our Cathedral couldn't be made fit for worship again in my life-time. But thank God, I am proved wrong.

1953

SWANSEA IN THE BLITZ

MALCOLM SMITH

Early this morning I saw some elderly men and women trudging through the streets clutching small cases and parcels in their hands. These were all they had left in the world, but many of them raised their hands and gave a cheery greeting. They were all quite determined that this sort of thing was not going to make any difference in the long run. The attitude of everyone here is just that, and there is no fear, and certainly no panic.

Mr. Attlee was here last Saturday and complimented Swansea on its Civil Defence Services, and our people on their courage. If he had been here last night and the night before he would have seen sights at which to marvel. Incendiary bombs were extinguished on roofs, in bedrooms, and sheds outside the houses, and indeed, anywhere and everywhere. In one case where an incendiary bomb had dropped in a bedroom the occupant extinguished it promptly, threw it out into the garden, and went immediately back to bed. A business man summed up our attitude in Swansea very aptly this morning when he displayed this notice on his bombed premises: "Bombed, Battered and Blitzed, but not Beaten." This notice could indeed be placed outside every damaged house and shop in Swansea today.

1941

116

PARLIAMENT IN WARTIME

Lady Megan Lloyd George

The main business of the week was the Prime Minister's statement and the debate on the war which did not, and yet did in the end, take place. Naturally, there was a good deal of expectation in the House and outside. Of course the Prime Minister would give an account of his journeying, he would make a survey but would he make any new declaration of policy? The House was crowded, members sitting huddled on the steps, some standing by the bar. I saw several Ministers tucked away modestly on the back benches among their lesser colleagues. Behind the Speaker's chair another group, among them Mr. Brendan Bracken with folded arms surveying the scene with the practised eye of the journalist. Up above the galleries were full, peers, ambassadors, members of the press.

The Prime Minister then flew us thirteen thousand feet up over the mountains and across long stretches of the Caspian Sea and so to Moscow and the meeting with Stalin. Here the Prime Minister gave us a characteristic and a brilliantly vivid character sketch of the Soviet leader. The rugged War Chief, a man of massive personality, suited to the sombre, stormy times in which his life had been cast; above all, a man with that saving sense of humour. It was about this point that members started to leave the chamber—before the end of the Prime Minister's speech. But when he had finished and Mr. Greenwood rose to speak, members rose in a body and poured out of the House pronouncing judgment loudly and vociferously until order was called for and there was only a thin sprinkling of members left on the benches.

1942

LLOYD GEORGE AT HOME

Lady Olwen Carey-Evans

Although we hadn't seen him, we knew there was something electric in the house, something had arrived, you know, and then we knew Father was there. And from that moment on he would entertain us. He was fun, he used to tell us all the stories like the Count of Monte-Cristo and the Hunchback of Notre Dame, all these and Dickens's Tales. That's how we learned them first before we read them, by Father telling us the stories. He loved the country and couldn't bear London really. We camped in Cwmstrachly which is just up above our house. We went out, tent and all, paraffin stove, and my brother Gwilym was there and my sister Megan, and I had friends staying with me, and we all went out camping. My mother had to go—she hated every minute of it.

She (*Dame Margaret Lloyd George*) was as calm as he was mercurial, and he would flap around sometimes and look for papers and everybody in the household would be rushing around looking for this speech that he had prepared. Where was it, and "What have you done with it?" Then she would appear very calmly and say "What is all this fuss about?" "Well," he said, "My papers, my papers." And then she'd disappear and she'd say "Are these the ones?" "Where were they, where were they?" Then he'd go off without saying one further word and then she'd just look at me and smile. She was a most wonderful person.

It wasn't always easy because he was very temperamental and very easily upset with little things, although he told us at one time that he was the most patient man in the world. We all smiled when he said that. He said "No, you're quite wrong you know", he said, "In politics I'm a very patient man." "Well", we said, "Not in your home, you're not!"

1963

THE PHENOMENON

HUBERT PHILLIPS

He was not one man but a phenomenon: a dozen men in one. His gifts of leadership and his positive achievements it is not necessary for me to stress: he made great constructive contributions both before 1914, when he changed the whole tenor of our social policy, and in World War I, when he made himself the embodiment of Britain's will to survive. Don't forget that twice—in 1917 and again in 1918—despair was not far round the corner. If, when victory had been achieved, Lloyd George's intuitions misled him, it was at least in large measure *his* victory. It was by intuition, rather than by the rationalisation of facts, that his mind worked. Some have called him an actor. Quite wrongly: he was the very opposite. A good actor must at all times see himself in his part objectively. In Mr. Lloyd George's approach to a person, or to a problem, a relationship, as it were, was instantaneously established, the fusion of Lloyd George's own personality with other elements. Such relationships might or might not prove stable, but I believe they were always genuine.

Two of his outstanding qualities are known to everyone: his personal charm—that is, I hope, implicit in what I have been trying to say—and his uncanny understanding of what was in other people's minds. You may recall Keynes's description of Lloyd George at Versailles: self-assured and dominant, where Woodrow Wilson was all at sea, "by the exercise of five or six senses not available to ordinary persons." Keynes was a great phrase-maker, but he hardly exaggerated here.

1948

119

A WARTIME MEETING

HUGH CUDLIPP

Just before the war I thought it would be a good idea to invite Mr. Lloyd George, who then was senior statesman, and in my opinion the greatest Prime Minister this country has ever had in this century, to write a weekly article about the war. This was in 1938 or 1939, and I went to see him at his rather splendid house in Churt.

At that time he was wearing—he was a great histrionic character as we all know—he was wearing a flowing gown and flowing white hair.

In fact everything was flowing including, if I remember at that particular meeting, the booze. Lloyd George gave me a great dramatic talk, walking around the room, flailing his arms around saying "I cannot write about the war because we cannot possibly win it. Tell me how we can live, how we can survive on the land, on the sea or in the air?"

He was a great defeatist at that time. But he did write articles which were not utterly defeatist and, of course, the tragedy of Lloyd George in the end was that he died just a few weeks before we did in fact win the war.

1976

LLOYD GEORGE AND WALES

MAJOR GWILYM LLOYD GEORGE M.P.

He was accused by some people of having neglected Wales once he became prominent in the public life of the nation. He resented this charge very much and at a meeting at Caernarvon to celebrate his 70th birthday he replied to it in his own inimitable way. It was one of the most moving things that I have ever listened to.

He likened himself to the river Severn, pointing out

120

that on its start from Plynlimon it was a tiny insignificant trickle and on its way through Montgomery it gathered strength, eventually finding its way into England, passing through Shropshire, Worcester and Gloucester, still gathering strength and rendering service now to England as well as Wales. Eventually in enters the Bristol Channel and there mighty ships of all countries of the world are carried on its bosom, but he said "What is the last thing it does? It turns back towards Wales before losing itself in the eternal sea." That is what he did.

1948

FATHER AND SON

T. Huws Davies M.P.

A number of Welsh members took part in the debates on the Address. Both priority and pride of place must be given to Mr. Gwilym Lloyd George who, in a most effective speech, moved the official Liberal amendment on the alleged lack of provision by the Government against a possible slump. For Matthew Arnold's sweet reasonableness commend me to his speech, and yet he was reared in the stormy petrel's nest.

Only two or three days previously the parent bird had demonstrated defiantly the unfailing strength and magnificent swoop of his wings amid the storms. Mr. Oliver Stanley made pretty use of the contrast.

"We have had the privilege during the last few days of hearing both father and son," he said. "All of us enjoyed the philippics of the elder, but the rather different style of the son does not suffer in comparison or effectiveness with the father. It is indeed refreshing to see them both, the father still young despite his years, and the other still moderate despite his example." There is no man living who can make any approximate assessment of the

121

father's gifts. We in Wales have known them in days of adversity and prosperity and have always wondered at and appreciated them. All those who come into contact with the son admire his courtesy, considerateness and charm, coupled with his unostentatious efficiency.

1938

THE BURNING ZEAL OF A YOUNG M.P.

T. I. ELLIS

Thomas Edward Ellis, the Liberal Member of Parliament for Merioneth, promised to be one of the most brilliant politicians of his time, something recalled here by his son T. I. Ellis. But T. E. Ellis died at the age of 40, before his abilities had been fully tested.

In 1886, two years after leaving Oxford, he could add the letters M.P. to his name. It is perhaps difficult for us, sixty years later, to realise what a portent this was. I use the word advisedly. He had come right out into the limelight: he had his chance, and he took it with both hands. For he began at once to regard Welsh interests and Welsh problems as his special concern.

Down to the Rhondda he went to help Mabon (*William Abraham, the Liberal M.P.)* in his campaign: on to Aberystwyth, and back to his own constituency, learning and teaching. And when the Parliamentary session began, he was instant in season and out of season. His maiden speech caught the ear of the House: his personal charm made him friends among Englishmen, Scotsmen, and Irishmen: he began to read Thomas Davis and Mazzini. "It is time for the Government to pay heed to the rights of Wales" was the burden of his work and his speeches: nothing that had to do with Wales did he deem foreign to him.

SIR HUGH CUDLIPP

BBC Wales

RT. HON MICHAEL FOOT

BBC Hulton Picture Library

Naturally the older Welsh members—men like William Rathbone, the Englishman who sat for the most Welsh division of Arfon, C. R. M. Talbot the Father of the House of Commons, W. R. H. Powell of Maesgwynne, and possibly Henry Richard,—began to feel disturbed and annoyed. Who was this young man, so charged with energy, so transparently sincere, so passionate in his desire for the betterment of Wales? They were used to leisurely, courtly, Victorian progress: he wanted things done, though he was no vulgar thruster. Gradually his efforts began to tell: and the people of Wales—his people—heard him more and more gladly. Tithe Riots in Denbighshire, Land Reform, Intermediate Education, the Church of England in Wales, even such matters as Sea Fisheries in Cardigan Bay: all these subjects and more, he took in his stride, and his burning zeal touched others among his fellows and inspired them to work and effort.

1948

N Y E

MICHAEL FOOT

The story is, in some respects, a tragic one. He should have been the Leader of the Party, he should have been Prime Minister, he should have had a chance to put all his ideas into full operation, and he was denied that and we were denied that, and I think that that was a political tragedy of the first order. I think that he expressed the ideas of democratic socialism better than any other socialist in Britain in this century, and I think that that was the fact was burnt into the minds of the people up and down the country, and many people in the great audiences up and down the country appreciated that maybe very often better than the politicians . . .

... He sometimes let loose great invectives against individuals although much more I think it was invective against a system and invective against the things he hated. Sometimes he could play with his opponents almost in a loving manner. I don't think he had much personal venom in him, but he could feel extremely angry, and I remember Jennie Lee saying to me on one occasion that Nye had said: "Well nobody knows how much violence I've got in me."

That violence he turned to constructive purposes but there's no doubt that he did have a very strong vibrant power within him that came out in his speech. But the idea that he as bitterly antagonistic to other individuals I don't think that was true, he could certainly give his opinions of them in colourful manner, but who objects to that?

1977

ODD PEOPLE

ARCHIE LUSH

We played a lot of billiards, this was probably the only release he had. Aneurin was quite a good billiards player. All he couldn't do was to win because I had more friends on the scoreboard than Aneurin had. We played billiards, we went for long walks, we talked for hours in a doorway in Tredegar late at night, and the police shone their lamps on us and came to the conclusion that if any revolution occurred they would probably book us at once. We were accepted as certain idiosyncracies, and that we were not normal in the normal sense of the word, we were just odd people ...

... He taught me the lesson that the danger was not the man, the danger was his ideas. People with the wrong ideas were our enemies not the persons themselves, but since the person epitomised the wrong ideas, in order to kill the idea it appeared that you killed the person. I

124

remember feeling a little worried during the war of his constant attacks on Churchill, and I remember his answer, and he said to me, "Suppose Churchill is knocked down by a bus tomorrow morning, do we write in to Hitler and tell him we've given in? The idea still has to go on that Hitler has to be defeated." And I think this is generally true, I can't remember any personal vendetta for any length of time with him, he'd come home angry about someone, or you'd meet him angry about something, but it was always because it was to him a stupid idea that the person was purveying.

1970

A POLITICAL PROMISE

OLIVER JONES

I really came into contact with him as a youth of seventeen. He was then a member of a Sunday School class—that Sunday School class I might tell you was more of a debating society. He was rather inclined to be critical of certain religious concepts. He had definite rationalist leanings. Aneurin and I clashed fairly often because he wasn't at all sympathetic to my metaphysical leanings at that time.

I remember one occasion when Aneurin had asked me to meet him and he took me for a long walk, a fine summer's day, but before we went he told me he had to make a call in one of the streets here called Iron Street. There a family had been suffering from unemployment for a long time. When we got there I found that he was making some enquiries as to the treatment these people were receiving by the Commissioners who had superseded the Guardians, and after a lot of questions and so on, he discovered that there was no food in the house. As it was a Saturday evening nothing could be done to get any help for these people. Aneurin took a note from his pocket and pushed it into the woman's hand and said, "Well, get something for the children."

When we came out of the house we strolled away, Aneurin taller than myself strode on furiously. I was trying to keep pace with him. Suddenly he stopped and I shot forward, going three or four paces before I realised he had stopped. When I turned back I saw the look on his face—it was one of fierce determination.

He said to me, "Oliver, I don't know how long I'm going to live, but I'm certainly going to make them pay for this before I finish."

1977

MOVING LEFT

MICHAEL FOOT

Michael Foot succeeded Aneurin Bevan as MP for Ebbw Vale in 1960.

I don't know that I've been an outsider exactly, because I was strongly in favour of sustaining the 1945 Labour Government. I backed it as strongly as I could, though we criticised it many times. It did some very fine things and some terrible things and some of us tried to sustain a democratic criticism inside the party then.

Then during the 1950s we had a great struggle to retain the idea of socialism in the Labour Party. If Gaitskellism had succeeded it would have driven the idea of effective change in society out of the Labour Party altogether. To some extent it succeeded. It succeeded in diminishing the allegiance to public ownership, in diminishing the idea of there is such a thing as a class struggle.

Gaitskellism undoubtedly had an effect in reshaping the Labour Party, which I think had highly disagreeable and melancholy consequences between 1964 and 1970. Nonetheless, I believe that our efforts, the Bevanites so-called, that we did succeed in saving this idea in the Labour Party and I think that these ideas are now coming back more into fashion. I don't say the Labour Party's taken an absolute lurch to the left but I think it's moving leftwards.

1973

DEMOCRACY AND PEACE

LADY RHONDDA

My father was a Radical, a peace lover and a democrat, and if there are two things which all my life I have believed in, they have been peace and democracy. There could be no more hopeless-seeming things to believe in today. My faith needs further qualification of course. Neither democracy nor peace are, as I see them ends in themselves, nor even necessarily desirable in themselves.

The quality of a democracy must depend on the quality, the sense of honour, the unselfishness, tolerance, kind-liness, courage, and on the degree of political education, insight and wisdom of the people who compose it. Obviously *bad* people could not make a good democracy. And the same arguments apply to peace. Peace which is founded on the genuinely peaceful inclinations, on the neighbourliness, kindliness and tolerance of a people, on their hatred of the terrible cruelty and brutality of war is a good peace. A peace that was founded on pure fear for themselves and used for purely material purposes, a peace that was merely another name for an opportunity for giving way to sloth and luxury, might very well be a bad peace. Do you remember, for example, what Ghandi, that great pacifist, replied when he was asked why he had enlisted men for service in the World War of 1914-18?

" . . . I do not believe" he said, "in the use of arms . . . it is contrary to the religion of Ahimsa which I profess . . . I do not believe in retaliation, but I did not hesitate to tell the villagers of Bettiah four years ago that they who knew nothing of Ahimsa were guilty of cowardice in failing to defend the honour of their women-folk and their property by force of arms. And I have not hesitated . . . to tell the Hindus that if they do not believe in out-and-out Ahimsa and cannot practise it, they will be guilty of a crime against their religion and humanity if they fail to defend by force of arms the honour of their women against any kidnapper who chooses to take away their women."

I have suggested that in addition to the possibility of there being different kinds of democracy and different kinds of peace there was also the fact, which I feel must always be borne in mind, that neither peace nor democracy are ends in themselves. They are merely the soil in which the most worthwhile things can grow. Without peace, without democracy, neither justice, freedom, tolerance nor equality between man and man can grow. I want to see a country (I have never seen one yet, though I have been in one or two small ones in the north of Europe which were a good deal nearer to my ideal than England yet is) in which the educational and economic and political equality of opportunity is the same for *all* men and women, and power is allowed only to those who have already proved to their fellow citizens' satisfaction that they can be trusted to use it solely for the common good. Then we shall have made a beginning—but even then only a beginning. We shall have made a soil in which the things that are worth having have a chance to grow and to bear fruit.

1938

COLONIAL FREEDOM

JAMES GRIFFITHS

As Minister of National Insurance in the 1945 Labour Government, James Griffiths, the MP for Llanelli, was one of the architects of the Welfare State. After the 1950 election he was given another crucial job.

When the second Attlee administration was formed in February 1950, there came another call to No. 10 and an invitation from Clem Attlee to join the Cabinet—and to become Secretary of State for the Colonies. On that first day at the Colonial Office, as I passed along the corridors to the Secretary of State's room I saw along the walls the portraits of former Secretaries of State—among them those of famous names in our political history. William Ewart Gladstone, Lord John Russell, Joseph Chamberlain, Winston Churchill and Sidney Webb.

On my desk I found a globe showing in red the fifty Colonies for which I would be responsible. Of all the offices I have filled, in and out of Parliament, this was the one that excited me most—that stirred the imagination and gripped the heart. My task was to guide the 70 million people in the Colonies towards responsible self-government within the Commonwealth, and to help them to lay the foundations of democratic independence by raising their living standards, promoting social progress and fostering the growth of democratic institutions. There have been other Empires, we read about them in our history books, of how they were founded, and grew and flourished, and then, of their decline and fall.

Britain in this mid-twentieth century has entered upon the great adventure of seeking to transform an Empire into a Commonwealth. One of the major decisions I made in my first year as Colonial Secretary was to introduce a new Constitution for the Gold Coast. And what a joy it was for me to be privileged to be at Accra on the 6th of this month to witness the birth of the new nation of Ghana. And to find Ghana, by its own choice, remaining with us in the Commonwealth and thus helping to create a community of nations in which people of different races, colours and creeds can live together in racial equality and human dignity.

This may well be the greatest contribution our country can make in this 20th century to the peace and progress of the world.

1957

WAITING FOR HAROLD

GEORGE THOMAS, VISCOUNT TONYPANDY

In 1964, when the Labour Party had won the election by a handful of votes, I thought that I was not going to get a job and I went to chapel on the Sunday morning. When I came in Mam said to me: "George, Number Ten has been on the telephone."

"Number Ten?" I said.

The request was, would I see the Prime Minister the next morning. I said I'd catch the night sleeper to London. What time did they want me?

"You're to go in the House of Commons and wait," they said. "You'll get a message when it's due for you to come over."

I was there at 7 o'clock in the morning and it was 7 o'clock at night before I had the telephone call to go over. When I went in I said, "Harold, do you realise I've been waiting all day?"

He got so annoyed. He said: "What do you think I've been doing? Wasting my time? I've been busy all day."

I said: "Well, I'm sorry."

He said: "Well, the job that we had for you is gone—that was Deputy Speaker.

I said: "You didn't get me all the way up from Cardiff to tell me that I'm not going to get a job, Harold?"

"No, I've got a very good job for you," he said.

"Have you?" I said. "What is it?"

"Well, it's a job that has need for compassion and kindness," he said.

"Oh," I said. "Is it National Insurance?"

He said: "No, that's arithmetic."

"Is it the Health Service?"

"No."

I said: "If you don't tell me Harold, I'll go up the wall and across the ceiling. What is it?"

"Parliamentary Under Secretary of State in the Home Office," he said, and my eyes opened.

"The Home Office—that's a great department of State, Harold."

"Yes, I know."

Then a few kind words and I was thrilled to be there.

He told me that we couldn't have the Deputy Speakership. The other side had offered to take it, to help the Government with one more vote. But the next Thursday I read in *The Times* that Major Anstruther Grey, the Deputy Speaker, decided that he wasn't going to take it.

I said to my Private Secretary: "Get me the Prime Minister on the telephone."

He looked at me as if I was out of my mind.

I said: "It's all right, he'll come for me."

Fair play, within a few minutes there was Gravel Voice, dear Harold, on the phone.

He said: "You've been reading *The Times*, have you George?"

"Yes, I can't understand it," I said.

He said, "Well, I told you the truth, we did have the offer that the other side would take the Deputy Speaker-

131

ship but they forgot to ask the man concerned and he didn't want to do it."

He then said to me these fateful words: "You can still have it if you want it, George."

I said: "Oh, no thank you Harold, I like being a Junior Minister."

Horace King took the job. Next year Mr. Speaker Hilton Foster dropped dead and Horace became Speaker. And that was ten years before I became Speaker of this House, so history is made on very simple things, isn't it?

1981

TRUTH GAMES

Patrick Hannan

Before he was virtually canonised, as he is now, Viscount Tonypandy was the political equivalent of a karate expert, delivering blows with both hands and feet. One election night he suddenly said to me—live, on television: "That is a very stupid question."

He was probably right, but it was considered to be a very shocking event, not least by his agent, who recognised that the public image was much more important than putting down some impertinent boy interviewer, however much he deserved it.

Much more in the traditional George Thomas-as-he-then-was style was his response to a question which inadvertently threatened to rip the packaging from some devious political ploy he was up to.

He paused briefly for thought and said: "That is a very *naughty* question," a phrase that gave him enough time to polish up some suitable non-answer. When the interview finished, we were both helpless with laughter, having realised that, for once, the truth had almost emerged.

1988

132

UNDERSTANDING NATIONALISM

Goronwy Rees

It is worth noticing that already there are some Welshmen willing to devote themselves heart and soul to the task of creating a nationalist movement, and it is almost certain they will succeed. At present their aims have none of the aggressive and destructive elements we associate with nationalism to-day. When I observe the indifference and stupidity with which Englishmen regard Welsh problems of culture and administration it seems to me that if they really wanted to create a nationalism of violence they could go no better way about it than they do. When, for instance, so eminently reasonable a demand as for a Secretary for Wales cannot even receive a serious hearing, it seems that the English have learned nothing from their mistakes in the past or from the violence outbreaks of nationalism that have swept Europe in recent years.

But perhaps you may think these speculations, so unlikely to be fulfilled that they have little relevance to the problems of Welshmen to-day, but in one sense at least they are relevant. Nationalist conflicts are certainly among the most serious that trouble the world to-day; and their outcome is certain to affect all Welshmen decisively whatever they think about them. Unless they are solved satisfactorily it seems certain that they must lead to war.

Yet most statesmen and politicians in their speeches and writings show such little understanding of what nationalist problems really are that there seems little hope they will ever come near to solving them. There are some who believe that only nationalist ambitions have any virtue and that in their name any cruelty and injustice may be done.

There are others who think that nationalist ambitions are to be condemned in all nations except one which possesses some mystical superiority over all others and for that reason has the right to oppress them. And there are others again who deny that nationalist aspirations have any value or validity whatever, and appear to believe that men will never be happy until suddenly translated into some international Utopia in which nations and nationalities have magically ceased to exist. There are few indeed who have the common sense to see that nationalism is an inevitable and necessary step to the creation of an international system, and for that reason above all is to be fostered and encouraged rather than distorted into forms that will prevent it ever reaching its proper end. Only when nations are able to do as they will with what is their own and no one else's will they be able or willing to join with each other in administering what they have in common.

It seems to me that the Welshman may have an important task to perform in helping to solve such problems. We are not a backward, a remote, or an uncivilized people. Through our industries in South Wales we are forced to keep abreast with the development of advanced nations. We do not labour under a sense of grievance or injustice, or think that hatred and violence are the only proper expression of our national feeling. Indeed we have a strong sense of belonging to an international community, as may be seen in the annual message sent by the children of Wales to the children of the world, or, in more remarkable forms, in the attempts of the Welsh miners to relieve the distress of their comrades in the Asturias or in the refuge given to the Basque children at Caerleon.

But at the same time we have preserved, even in the midst of industrialism, the sense of our national identity, our native culture, our native language, and our native institutions, and we have created new institutions as remarkable as those we have inherited. Our form of life is genuinely democratic and equalitarian, far more so than in England. It seems to me that, in such conditions, it should be possible for us to create in theory and in practice, a form of nationalism which in essence should contain the solution to the acute nationalist conflicts of to-day.

1938

SELF-AWARENESS

RICHARD HUGHES

The big change affecting the nation, as I see it, has been a shift in emphasis. Don't misunderstand me if I call it a shift from cultural to political nationalism. By 'culture' I don't mean just books and pictures and music, the language controversy and Dylan Thomas. And when I say 'political' I am not just thinking of elections and political parties, Home Rule and Secretaries of State. What I mean is that there has been a distinct shift in Wales from *being* a peculiar nation to *saying* that we are a peculiar nation. Instead of talking Welsh as a matter of course, people now talk about talking Welsh; instead of being Welsh as a matter of course, we now talk about being Welsh. It's only when the confident swimmer gets his first twinge of cramp that he begins to struggle, and thinks how horrible it would be to drown.

1950

DEVOLUTION

PATRICK HANNAN

*This talk was broadcast exactly a year before the Labour
Government's Devolution proposals which included plans for
an elected Welsh assembly were comprehensively defeated in a
referendum.*

I was going to suggest that the emblem of this Government
should be the leek but since that might be misunderstood
I'd better make it the daffodil instead. As such it would
represent the remarkable dominance exerted by Welsh-
men in the Cabinet and at other levels of Government.
The Prime Minister, who of course represents a Welsh
seat, is fond of suggesting that it's England that should
be looking for independence since he and his Welsh
colleagues form such a powerful lobby. Mr. Michael
Foot, for instance, inherited Nye Bevan's seat in Ebbw
Vale, and some of the adulation that went with it.
The Lord Chancellor was born in Llanelli, the Home
Secretary in Cilfynydd. Dr. David Owen—David Anthony
Llewellyn Owen, indeed, has strong Welsh connections
and two of his Ministers of State at the Foreign Office are
Welsh. Of the 22 Welsh Labour MPs, half hold office in
this Government. And the Speaker, Mr. George Thomas,
sometimes seems to be the living embodiment of the
Rhondda. In other circumstances such outrageous
power-grabbing by a closely-knit group of politically-
motivated men would be considered a dangerous
conspiracy.

So it comes as something of a surprise to hear people
suggesting that the Government is really interested only
in devolution for Scotland since that's where the political
pressure comes from. In fact it might have been relatively
easy to ditch the plans for a Welsh assembly at a number
of stages without running a great risk of electoral disaster
in Wales. It could have been done tactfully, with a

promise of something for Wales in the following year, but the Government has been more determined to keep both measures going than many people anticipated. The close links that Government has with Wales make it more sensitive to the reaction of the Labour Party in Wales and to that of the trade unions who form a political pressure group in favour of an elected assembly.

Indeed, the Wales TUC is currently so incensed with Labour backbenchers voting against the Government on devolution that officials are muttering darkly about withdrawing support from such members. And this week they met the Scottish TUC to consider such matters jointly.

The Government also recognises the moral force of the case put forward by the Labour Party in Wales, based on the fact that the party was calling for an elected assembly when nationalist MPs were just a twinkle in a psephologist's eye. Among those doing the demanding was Mr. Foot, which is why he now insists that devolution is not a cynical response to a purely political problem.

The test of the Government's goodwill, though, won't be so much in the progress of the Wales Bill through Parliament: the Scottish example shows clearly that where backbenchers are determined to make changes, Ministers and Whips can do little except close their eyes and think of England. The test will come instead in the promised referendum.

This week the Wales for the Assembly Campaign, which has been in mothballs for the last year, re-launched itself with rousing pledges to fight those who would wreck devolution. In conversation after their press conference it became clear that many of the campaigners believe that in the referendum it could be the Government's strength of purpose that could be the deciding factor.

In particular they feel that if Mr. Callaghan were willing to stand at the hustings and put his personal authority behind a vote in favour of a Welsh assembly it would go a long way towards drawing out the level of support they need. But on the other side those who oppose devolution are hoping that Ministers who disapprove of the policy will be free to state the case for a 'no' vote.

Such matters will make the referendum in Wales perhaps the most complicated political campaign we've yet seen in this country. The Labour Party in Wales, and elsewhere, is divided. The Liberals support an elected assembly but they really want federalism. Plaid Cymru, the Welsh Nationalist Party, wants self-government for Wales but seems to be generally—although not unanimously —in favour of devolution as a first step in that direction. But Plaid Cymru also has to decide whether a campaign in favour of an assembly would be to its advantage since it could well identify devolution with nationalism and thus persuade many people to vote against. The pro-devolution lobby fears that the result might be influenced by CBI money coming from England, despite the fact that the CBI as an organisation has never been notably flush, but some industrialists may not be anxious to be so closely identified with the Conservative Party which, in Wales at least, is vigorously against any elected assembly.

To put the question another way, could Mr. Neil Kinnock of the Tribune Group stand on the same platform as Mrs. Thatcher and condemn devolution? Or could Mr. Callaghan and Mr. Gwynfor Evans, the Plaid Cymru President, for once stand shoulder to shoulder and fight for the same cause? St. David was the most noted of Welsh teetotallers: even he might have thought a drink was necessary to resolve such issues.

1978

VICOUNT TONYPANDY

GWYN JONES

BBC Wales

PLANNING THE FUTURE

EDWARD NEVIN

In September 1965 the Department of Economic Affairs produced its National Plan—intended as a centrepiece in the strategy to be followed by the Labour Government which had been elected the previous year.

Now, people react to the word 'planning' in different ways, but even if you are one of those who reaches for his gun at the very sound of the word, the fact has to be faced that the appearance of this plan is a very important event for this country in general, and Wales in particular, for good or ill according to your taste in these matters. For the first time a conscious effort is being made to shape the long term development of this country in a deliberate, definite way, and to bring out into the open the basic policy decisions which have to be taken if that development is to be as rapid as is possible for it to be.

In the past we have suffered pretty badly in this country from our habit of living from hand to mouth, from oscillating between twelve or eighteen months of boom and bust and another twelve months of restrictions and cuts and wage pauses and smoking brake drums in general.

You couldn't run a whelk stall properly on that sort of basis and it is hardly surprising that in the odd moments when we have been able to lift our eyes from the hiccups in our domestic economy, we invariably find that the Germans, the French, the Italians and all the rest have been leaving us way behind.

The fact that the Continentals are showing us a clean pair of heels probably isn't important in itself except to our national ego. But what is important is that if our productive capacity hasn't expanded as rapidly as it could have done, well then, we've denied ourselves the opportunity to improve the lot of the underprivileged members of our society or to build decent schools or hospitals or roads, or to give under-developed countries something more than the miserable pittance they've had from us in recent years.

There's so much to be done, so many things badly needed by so many people despite all our talk about the affluent society. And it is not our job to let opportunities of doing some of these things drift past us by lack of thought. Now this, I think, is the essential philosophy of the (Economic) plan—the idea that if nationally we all get together and agree in a general way on our broad objectives, if we exchange information about our intentions and proposals, well then, there is at least a chance that possible bottlenecks or shortages can be seen ahead and something done about them, that individual industries are a little clearer about both their future supplies and their future markets, can arrange their expansion programmes with more confidence and that the Government can take action in time to insure the required foundation for industrial growth—labour, power, communications, and so on, is provided at the necessary time and in the necessary places.

1965

THE SURVIVAL OF WELSH

Gwyn Jones

The reasons why all thinking men will hope for the health and survival of the language are many and incontrovertible. They range from such vast abstractions as the relation between language (and therefore languages) and the width and depth of mankind's culture and civilisation, and the totality of his experience, to the inalienable right of a man to express his thought, clothe his emotions, and fill out his actions with the language of his choice.

Under these heads there is no room for debate. I accept them without qualm or quibble. As I accept the reinforcing arguments of the antiquity of the Welsh tongue, its literary heritage (whose substance belongs to us all), its decisive role in nationhood and nationalism. On the personal level I acknowledge as truth that a Welshman without Welsh suffers loss and diminution; and that even if, as in the majority of cases, this troubles him little or not at all, no one among us should seek by action or deliberate inaction to inflict that loss and diminution on any man alive or child unborn.

But you are thinking, with justification, that none of these fine sentiments will of itself preserve the Welsh language not only into eternity but into the next century. It will be kept alive by use, nothing else. Does this make me an optimist or a pessimist? Neither. A realist. Which means a bit of both.

I believe that the speakers and writers of Welsh, the true living repositories of the language, will keep it as fully in use, and as fully alive, into the twenty-first century as they have done in this the twentieth. I do not believe that Welsh will ever again become the first language of Wales. That battle has been lost, if it ever took place. Nor do I believe that Wales will become a bilingual country. It is a hundred years too late for that. The Welsh-speaking minority will perforce remain bilingual. The English-speaking majority, a big one, will stay English-speaking. This not over-cheerful view of things I have tried to keep untinged by emotion, though I understand with what emotion—indeed, emotions—the subject is charged. Call it, if you like, the best guess I can make as to the future. English, by the linguistic accident of the American succession, is determined and, as I think, irresistibly on the increase: but the Celtic languages, like a great many other beautiful and desirable things, are not what English now calls growth-points. The natural sloth and cultivated inertia of English-language users in respect of all languages save their own is being powerfully and unhandsomely confirmed. Also, green paper and whitewash notwithstanding, the theory and practice of agglomerative egalitarian education are more conducive to the production of half-literates in one language than masters of two. More generally the modern holy grails of size, increase and bigger-is-better-than-big are inimical to difference and distinction. Small may be beautiful, but assuredly it is not big—and what profit cometh out of Nazareth? And at the bottom end of the ladder most Welsh-language campaigns will provoke counter-action, on the ground, at once ironic and natural, of fair play for all, or 'Every man for himself', as the elephant said when he danced among the chickens.

If then I am right (and I could well be wrong) the language situation at the end of the century will be very much what it is today. But if I am wrong (and I could very well be right), and the Welsh language has experienced a further stage of decline, retreated into enclaves, become an academic relict, would that mark the end of the Welsh nation and of Welshness? Most assuredly not.

Let me in this be as clear as I can. The disappearance or severe contraction of Welsh as a living tongue would be a national and human disaster, and to many Welshmen it *would* be the end of Wales—their Wales. If I thought it would emphasise that to say it a second time, I would say it even a third. But Ireland is very much Ireland despite the failure of recent attempts to make Irish a living, everyday and all-Ireland tongue. And Scotland, despite the breast-beaters and sporran-baiters, is emphatically Scotland. Wales will still be Wales. Any other belief is the product of or prelude to despair. I have been saying since 1939 that Welshness and the Welsh language are not synonymous, so I am saying nothing new or unexpected if I say it again. Even so I am saying it in a new context. The earlier one was a rebuttal of the notion that the English-speaking Welshman of South Wales was no

Welshman. That no longer needs to be said. My present context would be altogether more alarming, save for one thing. It is a hypothesis, which serves to illustrate an actuality. That actuality is that a Welshman is a Welshman even before he is a Welsh speaker. It is a noteworthy thing that Pennar Davies and Bobi Jones should turn to the Welsh language and become distinguished Welsh poets. But had they not done so, clearly they would have become distinguished Anglo-Welsh poets. In terms of my present argument, either way they are Welshmen and members of the family.

Which brings me back to where I started—or did I?: the role of the English-speaking Welsh. But permit me one necessary and unfacile repetition. Warmly, gladly and from the heart, and with a full sense of my personal insignificance, and even irrelevance in this context, I believe that the Welsh language will survive all the trials and tribulations that will surely beset it, and enrich for ever the lives of its daily users and—a selfish but monitory thought—the existence of all Welshmen everywhere.

1977

A LOVELY PARTY

SAUNDERS LEWIS

In 1962 the playwright Saunders Lewis gave his radio lecture Tynged yr Iaith *which was the inspiration for the founding of Cymdeithas yr Iaith Gymraeg, the Welsh Language Society, and was thus one of the origins of a whole series of campaigns on behalf of Welsh language issues. In the previous year Lewis had addressed some of the same issues in an English talk.*

I know all the Welsh education authorities are kidding themselves that a bilingual Wales is an excellent ideal and a possibility. I think it is just not true. It is only the Welsh-speaking people of Wales that you can make bilingual and they will only be bilingual for a transition period. Once all the monoglot Welsh are gone the bilingual Welsh will quickly turn monoglot English. We are now in the transition period. For a young writer it is an unhappy predicament. Dr. Kate Roberts has recently deplored the degenerate idiom of our younger writers and of their society. It hasn't got the raciness of phrase, the sureness of syntax, the gift of noun-making, that come naturally to a living monoglot community. English idiom enters unconsciously into Welsh speech today. It is all about us, in radio set and television screen and newspaper. Inevitably there's a landslide of deterioration.

Yet I don't think the rot has gone too far to be checked. The surprising thing is that there's a kicking life in the young Welsh writers of today. Stranger still, some of the most fertile and prominent among them have learnt Welsh at school or college or later and have set themselves to write in Welsh like professionals. I think of a German lady, an Egyptologist and classical scholar, possessing also the German literary tradition from the eighteenth century to Thomas Mann, who has written novels and short stories and essays in Welsh and has in journalism published her own first-hand impressions of post-war Eastern Germany and Russia.

Others of these are poets, novelists, dramatists; in Llangefni, in Aberystwyth, in Llandeilo, in Swansea, some of them with a quite turbulent abundance of output. Why did they choose Welsh and just at this time of day? Did they fall in love with it? Perhaps it was love, but I think they would also, if pressed, say to the Welsh language:

> I could not love thee, dear, so much,
> Loved I not honour more

There's a cavalier gaiety about the kissing of these new writers. You say we're for the dark, that our language is doomed? Alright my bonny, be it so, and how long is your own expectation of life? At any rate we, here in Wales, will make it the end of a lovely party.

1961

TWO TONGUES

PROFESSOR ALUN DAVIES

My upbringing was, of course, a bilingual one. And I must say that I have always reckoned this to have given me a tremendous advantage. I couldn't speak English until I was eight years old. Thereafter, I have always deliberately sought every opportunity to speak my native tongue. Bilingualism is a most important topic with us in Wales these days. We are all reading and talking about the Gittins report on primary education—our Welsh equivalent of the Plowden report. And the Gittins report has come out quite firmly and unequivocally for a bilingual education. It's been quite amusing to watch the reactions to it. For example, such a responsible newspaper as *The Times* adopted a most high and mighty attitude to the proposition, and drew completely erroneous and irrelevant parallels between the Welsh language and the Irish language. But be that as it may. The point is that the very mention of 'bilingualism' immediately raises political overtones, and that in the most shrill way. If you talk in favour of a bilingual education you are immediately assumed to be a member of *Plaid Cymru*, the Welsh political nationalist party.

This, of course, is rubbish. And for my own part, I not only rejoice but am most indebted to the fact that I am bilingual, I have always found it to be a tremendous education. To be able to begin to appreciate, however dimly, from an early age that there exists a culture other than the English has always been to me an inestimable boon.

Indeed, I have heard it argued that in order to be a social anthropologist, you *must* have knowledge of more than one culture. To take some examples: Professor Fleure, one of the founding fathers of the modern science of anthropology was a Channel Islander, and equally at home in both French and English; Malinowski was a Pole; Raymond Firth is a New Zealander; Max Gluckmann is a South African. It's an interesting thesis.

However this may be, all I can say is that when I came to learn foreign languages, and to begin to probe into alien cultures, I found my bilingualism a tremendous advantage. For example, I had been brought up on the Welsh *englyn*—a traditional four-line poem which is constructed according to certain rules. When I came to learn Japanese, I came across the *tanka*—a verse of thirty-one syllables, also constructed according to certain rules. It is, perhaps, best known to Westerners because Richard Mason used a line from this poem as the title of one of his best-sellers, *The Wind Cannot Read*.

Bilingualism is only the beginning. There is also the use of words. We Welsh are often accused of being prodigal with words. In the countryside, we usually approach subject which are in any way personal in a very round

146

about way. Direct questions play a much smaller part than in modern urban and industrial life. Usually, if we call upon a neighbour to ask a favour of him, we lead the conversation up all sorts of highways and byways before coming to the point. This exposes us to the accusation of hypocrisy, but if you know the game, it's quite a fascinating one to play. When I started to learn an Oriental language, I found the circuitous approach not unfamiliar. I also found that in eastern countries, too, much entertainment and recreation was derived from story telling. Just as in rural Wales before the advent of radio and television, we listened avidly to long and sometimes involved tales, so did Indians gather around as dusk was falling, to listen to tales and legends.

1968

LINGUISTIC ANARCHY

GORONWY ROBERTS M.P.

It is a curious fact that while there is a discernible common factor in the approach of all Welsh Local Education Authorities to the teaching of French or German, and an utter uniformity of approach to the teaching of English, their attitude to the teaching of the native tongue of Wales is marked by anarchical diversity. Indeed, there are few counties in Wales which can claim to have anything like a coherent policy for the teaching of Welsh even within their own borders.

Now, I don't believe that you can force any authority to teach or any child to learn the Welsh language in any given way or indeed at all. But I am equally of the opinion that it is the duty of us all in Wales—all of us—to co-operate in preserving and spreading the Welsh language and cultural modes in literature, music, and society to which it is the key.

I know that I am speaking to many who know no Welsh and who perfectly sincerely may regard the language as useless and redundant. Let we warmly appeal to you to join in the effort to preserve in the sum of this battered world's culture the unique element which the language of Wales contributes. May I put it this way? Whatever may be your own attitude to the language, isn't it common fairness to give every child in Wales the opportunity of learning it and of entering into the rich world of though and expression through its doorway?

1948

LONDON LEARNING

IFOR EVANS

I can recall very vividly as a small boy right in the centre of London before I went to school learning Welsh as a first language, and finding even a sense of strangeness and bewilderment when I began for the first time to move about among English boys and to begin to try and learn my lessons in a language which to me was strange.

I can still remember the Welsh classes that my brother and I used to attend every Friday night and the bribe that my father would offer if we made good progress of a seat at the Wild West Film next door to the Chapel Hall where the classes were held. All that by the way was back in the happy days when a film seat cost threepence. Indeed my early memories of the Welsh language in London are mixed with the pictures of cow-boys moving jerkily to incredible adventures on a blurred screen.

1951

CENSUS

J. PARRY LEWIS

The census of 1951 revealed some unexpected—and disturbing—facts about the state of the Welsh language.

In Glamorganshire there are about 4,000 people who speak Welsh but no English. In Caernarvonshire, one person in nine cannot speak English, but about three in nine speak no Welsh. In all about 50,000 Welsh people speak no English, i.e., roughly two Welshmen in every hundred.

Is Welsh dying? We can get a good idea of the answer to this question if we look at the numbers who speak Welsh at different ages. They are not a complete guide, because they do not allow for migration in and out of Wales, but they give us a pretty good idea. Of the children in Wales aged 3 or 4 on Census Day, 13 in a hundred spoke Welsh. Of those aged between 5 and 9, about 20 in a hundred spoke it. The next groups, aged 10 to 14 and 15 to 24 had roughly the same proportion, the latter group showing a slightly larger proportion of Welsh speakers. But of those aged between 25 and 64, about 30 in 100 spoke Welsh, while of those aged 65 and over the figure is 40 in a hundred. These are figures that speak for themselves. Welsh is a language of old men. Unless some great change of policy occurs, it seems unlikely that as much as a fifth of our population will be speaking Welsh in another thirty years time . . . and even that is probably optimistic. It is up to the schools and the B.B.C. and, above all, to Welsh-speaking parents.

1953

ARTIFICIAL RESPIRATION

KINGSLEY AMIS

*Kingsley Amis is notably sarcastic about public attempts
—like bilingual signs—to promote the Welsh language.*

It's too late, a long time too late. There probably never
was a time when there was a clear time to stand up and
resist. How do you resist? How do you organise people to
do what? What does resisting mean anyway? But, when a
language ceases to be a daily thing and the common coin
of everyday life, it's dead; and that's the case over very
large parts of Wales now—more so, of course, than when
I first came to Wales in 1949.

I think it is worse to try and revive it artificially than to
leave things as they are. The only recourse is to study a
dead literature, or a very nearly dead literature, as a very
valid and interesting academic subject: to study it, not to
try and revive it or base anything in present life upon it.

1987

REAL POETRY

SIR IDRIS BELL

The Welsh are no doubt a more emotional, temperamental,
excitable people than the English, but, like the French,
whom in several ways they resemble, they have usually in
their poetry shown a preference for the classical rather
than the romantic. They have always tended to lay special
emphasis on rule and prescription, on formal perfection,
on fidelity to tradition and convention, and the avoidance
of individual eccentricity. To the bardic schools, which
dominated Welsh poetry down to the beginning of the
seventeenth century and whose influence still survives,
poetry is less an individual impulse, as it appears to most

Englishmen than a social function, not an uncovenanted inspiration but a craft to be learned as one learns any other craft.

It is the prevailing idea in England that anyone who is sufficiently articulate can write poetry, or at least passable verse, with no special preparation; but the Welshman who attempts to compose an *englyn* or a *cywydd* without a lengthy schooling in the Welsh metrical system merely makes himself ridiculous.

In the Middle Ages the aspirant to poetic distinction went to school with some bard of standing, the craft being handed on from master to pupil for generations in a sort of apostolic succession; today he consults one of the standard treatises on Welsh metrics. That by the late Sir John Morris Jones, for example, contains no less than 382 pages. So deeply engrained in the Welsh poetic consciousness is this idea that poetry is essentially a craft, subject to strict rules, that in the eighteenth century we find Goronwy Owen, a fine poet in the traditional manner and an even finer critic, denying the name of poetry to the more loosely textured verse of England, and saying of Milton's "Paradise Lost" (for which he expressed great admiration), "You will find me ready to subscribe to anything that can be said in praise of it, provided you do not call it poetry."

1947

UNHAPPY CHRISTMAS

WIL IFAN

We were not too sophisticated to appreciate the most homely gift and the gay Christmas card; and to prove to you how utterly unspoilt we were. I confess that we even read the very rhymes on the cards!

In recent years that particular joy has been filched from

me, by my own foolishness. An English firm of publishers specialising in Christmas cards approached me about supplying them with sets of suitable verses. The person who had suggested my name to them evidently had his own idea of my poetic standards.

At any rate I was tempted and I fell. Little did I think that these cards would find their way, year by year, to the counters of our popular multiple firms and that thus many of the printed greetings I receive are just my own anonymous words thrown back at me as just retribution. That is why I prefer the old stereotyped straightforward greeting:—"A Merry Christmas to you!" *"Nadolig Llawen!"*

1945

DISAPPEARING WALES

ALUN RICHARDS

Careful though we must be not to romanticise, the spirit of place survives irrespective of language, and it is perhaps this sense of deriving from somewhere different, of being apart even in one's own country, that gives even the stumbling writer some of the drive that is necessary to write at all. Unfettered by the chains of the past, by the apparently ageless language and drink arguments that persist elsewhere, the South Walian today is free of these things. He has no need to be selfconscious, to wear his cap with a difference, or even to trail the Celtic twilight. He is in the middle of, and has easy access to, problems that beset people everywhere, that are not specifically Welsh, that demand all he has to give as a writer—and—this is the hardest bit—can provide him with no excuses if he fails.

For if he writes in English, he must stand the competition of writers everywhere and grin and bear it. For him at any rate, there is not the advantage of shelter under a local rock, and perhaps this is not a good thing either. A literature is not made up only of those who succeed only in the face of the most merciless competition.

It is made up of the sum total of what is written at a given time and perhaps this is why dramatists, for example, from small countries or clearly defined localities, seem invariably to amass a substantial body of work without the discouragement that faces those who are led to compete in fields of strictly commercial entertainment.

Fortunate is the writer, said Saunders Lewis in another connection, who has his own square mile. It is true in more senses than one, but it has its disadvantages also. James Joyce's proposition, 'Ireland is an old sow that eats her own farrow', needs re-examining. On the whole, it is up to the farrow what they make of the sow, or whether even, they accept her as such.

For myself, and I suspect, for most people of my generation to whom the nonconformist tradition, the Welsh Language, Sabbath Day Observance, the morality of having bars in Welsh university colleges, are part of a past that is not even thought about let alone discussed. But this does not mean that we are lost as some of our elders tell us. It means that our important problems are no longer special. What is happening in Wales is happening everywhere. Large scale units of production, the increasing centralisation of industry and the creation of suburban dormitory towns where once individual communities flourished—this is what is happening now.

In so many ways, the Wales even of my childhood has changed and is changing. The supermarket, the mobile shop, the trading estate, the colossal steel mill, the widespread use of hire-purchase facilities, even the increased incidence of car ownership have changed the habits of people in a way that has yet to be fully understood or written about. If we face the affluent society

—its advantages and its ugly underside—with a more deeply entrenched suspicion than other areas, it is because of our past—a past, it should be stated, that begins with the industrial revolution and the concentration of one major industry, at the expense of others.

Today, there is not the same dependence on one industry, but as a result, there is not the same common bond between workers in different industries, or the feeling for place common to people whose home and place of work are the same. And this perhaps, is a far greater loss than the Welsh language, for there is nothing more hideous than the dormitory town, nothing more anti-life than the suburban squalor and anonymous isolation of cosy collections of houses whose inhabitants feel no common identity.

When this happens everywhere—as it has happened to a considerable extent in, say, Cardiff for example, then there will not be the opportunity to examine borrowed Irish phrases of abuse at leisure. We may still squabble about the causes, but all around us will be the evidence of final oblivion, and if the English suburban experience is anything to go on, we will have few distinctive writers either.

1963

A MEDIUM-SIZED POET

Dannie Abse

I often wonder why it is that chairmen at poetry readings never introduce a poet simply as a poet. The description "poet" always has to be qualified. "We have here today, ladies and gentlemen, a *young* poet." Which means that that physical wreck of a man with long hair and a lilac coloured tie on the platform is aged under 45. If he

154

G V WYNNE JONES

BBC Wales

RICHARD BURTON
BBC Broadcasting House London W1

happens to be older, then he is introduced as one of our "younger poets."

I have on occasions stood on that platform myself, having been pressurised into giving a poetry reading. In Hampstead, London, I have been introduced as a "Hampstead poet." Fair enough. I once lived in Hampstead. In Golden Green I have been labelled "a Golders Green poet." Well, I happen to live there now. In Cardiff I'm called "a Cardiff poet", which I suppose is reasonable since I was born there. In Swansea I'm introduced as "a Welsh poet." Cardiff, after all, officially, is the capital of Wales, and my mother was born in Ystalyfera and my father comes from Bridgend. So "Welsh poet" is not entirely an illegitimate description. If I should happen to be talking to, say, The Anglo-Jewish Society, then I'm happily introduced as that "young Jewish poet"—and Jewish I am, certainly. I'm waiting, now, for some nippy chairman to announce me as that 5 foot 8½ inches poet. Ah well, it's all very confusing, and of course, flattering. It's nice to be wanted. Thank-you all. But sometimes I look at my own poetry and wonder if any of these qualifications, Jewish and Welsh, particularly have any relevance to my work. Is there, in fact, such a thing, say as Anglo-Welsh poetry? And, if there is, should I be included in anthologies committed to that category of verse? For a start, let me take a poem at random, say my most recent poem, and examine it from that point of view. It happens to be called, *Sunday Evening*.

> Loved not for themselves those tenors who sing
> arias from "Aida" on horned tinny
> gramophones—but because they take a man back
> to a half forgotten thing.
>
> We, transported by this evening loaded
> with a song recorded by Caruso,
> recall some other place, another time,
> now charmingly outmoded.

What, for wrong motives, too often is approved
proves we once existed—becomes more flattery
—then it's ourselves whom we are listening to,
and by hearing we are moved.
&
To know, haunted, this echo too will fade,
with the alliteration of the leaves
and indistinct rain that drags down the sky
like a sense of gloom mislaid.

Dear classic, melodic absences
how stringently debarred, kept out of mind,
till some genius on a gramophone
holes defences, breaks all fences.

What lives in a man and calls him back
and back through desolate Sunday evenings?
Indescribable, oh faint generic name:
sweet taste, bitter lack.

The poem harks back certainly to Sundays of years ago,
and up to the age of eighteen I spent all my Sundays in
Wales. Some people, music hall comics among them, say
that Welsh Sundays are different from English Sundays
but this isn't revealed in my poem. If that was the subject
matter then it might, tolerably, be called an Anglo-Welsh
poem. As it stands, it is not. On the other hand, I have a
suspicion that if I entitled it "Sunday evening in Cardiff",
or "Sunday evening in Ystrad Mynach" then, if it were
good enough, it would soon be included in some Anglo-
Welsh anthology or poetry. I think we should beware of
Anglo-Welsh mongering and recognise topographical
fraud for what it is. Certainly poets anywhere are rare
enough and it might be sad to omit good poets like Dylan
Thomas and Vernon Watkins from an Anglo-Welsh
anthology simply because they haven't, or only rarely, use
Welsh furniture in the hotels of their poems where

156

people go in and out and live for a while. For it seems to me that a poem about a magpie seen in Wales is no different basically from a poem about a magpie seen in England, and a love poem is unlikely generally, to have a Welsh connotation if written in English by a Welshman. To put it another way: I don't think there is such a thing as a specific Anglo-Welsh style or tone, and that the Welshness of an English poem simply depends on what the poem is about.

1960

THE WORKING-CLASS WRITER

B. L. COOMBES

There is still a very deep pit between the mass of workers in this country and the intellectuals. It is that pit that we, the working-class writers, are trying to bridge. We are suited for the task because our own folk trust us, and they feel we may be able to portray their lives in a way that those on the other side of the pit can understand. We are not spectators looking on at the battle for a living; we are in that battle. If our writings are sometimes crude and unpolished, it is the conditions—not ourselves—that are to blame. I believe there is a most urgent need for many more workers in the mine, in the factory, in the foundry, or on the farms to study the craft of writing and become our helpmates in bridging this gap of ignorance which divides the people.

But if we are going to be craftsmen we must study our craft. There is no excuse for presenting badly written work—nor any hope of its being accepted when it's presented. We must improve our grammar; but not to the extent that the fear of making an error dominates our writing. We must learn how to observe and record—how to look harder and deeper into every happening until we see and feel the marrow of it—something that the others have missed. Our work needs to be well written so that it will give some pleasure to those who are trained in the value of words. But it needs to be written so naturally that the most halting reader among our own class will not be puzzled by difficult wording or involved phrasing.

I decided one day to give all my spare time during two years to the study of words and the way writers use them. I did so, and began writing. But it was nearer four years before I gained the first encouragement. I forget how many pens and pencils I wore out or how many copy books I filled. Each story I sent out I thought was a masterpiece—but they came back. Then I had to study the reasons for that return. Were there enough dialogue or action? Did the opening sentence attract the reader? Did the ending satisfy? Or had I sent it to the wrong magazine? I found that studying the market was as important as anything.

I began to realise that each branch of writing had its own method and technique. The short story, for instance, has no room for the waste word or the unnecessary situation. Yet a mere anecdote of a couple of hundred words isn't a short story. In the novel you can ramble a bit, but I found that the writing and revising of a short story of some hundred thousand words, maintaining my own interest, and my reader's all the while, was no small task. My enthusiasm and temper usually got a little frayed before I got halfway and those things show in the writing.

It is in the factual article about his industry that the worker-writer will find his brightest prospect. He has an intimate knowledge of the work and once he can express what he knows he finds editors eager for his material. He is right in the hub of his particular industry, and he can give the world a knowledge of what goes on far away from its sight—and the world want to know.

He has the great advantage of knowing what is happening each day, for our industries don't stand still—their problems change every year and sometimes more often than that. As one instance, take the mining industry; an industry where the workers spend one third of their life hidden away from daylight and the pleasant things of this world. They burrow, like moles, using artificial lighting and breathing forced air.

On what happens in those underground workings depend the welfare of the wives and children who wait above in the mining valleys—and the shopkeepers and professional men who live by the mining communities. If you, a working-class writer, leave the valleys and live for one year away from them—say in London—their lives and thoughts will fade from among your closest memories, and in that interval many fresh problems will have arisen, which you know nothing about. Many a working-class writer has been ruined by going away from the only life he knows anything about, and trying to live on his mental capital. You won't catch me leaving my valley.

1947

TERRIBLE

RICHARD HUGHES

If there's a play or a book or a film supposed to depict us we flock to it in hundreds: and then out we come, shaking our heads at each other—"Terrible! Terrible!"—Honestly, have you ever heard a Welshman have a good word for anything of general appeal ever written about modern Wales? Caradog Evans? We chased him out of the country. Dylan Thomas? The fame of his poetry is worldwide, and he's a prince among story-tellers; but have *we* . . . well, accorded him even the most minor national bardic honours? No fear!—That prose book of his, re-living his life as a boy in Swansea—Gower— Llanstephan—it's *peerless* in its penetration into South

159

Wales character—Terrible! Terrible! (My *word* it's good!).

What is the Welshman who takes to his pen to do, then? Write about the English, or the Red Indians? Set his scene in Timbuctooting? If he does we call him a renegade, not worthy of the name of Welshman. Write about his neighbours as *he* sees them, then (or even as *he* would like to see them)? "Terrible, Mrs. Cadwaladr, *terrible!*" . . . Write about his neighbours as they see themselves?— D'you know the kind of hand-tinted photograph of herself a girl likes to send to her young man's aunt in Canada, who there's no fear will ever meet her? Do we want that?

Suppose and suppose . . . suppose a fairy did grant to every one of us the gift of looking like exactly whatever he wanted to look like. Not only you—you'd make yourself look very distinguished and interesting, I've no doubt— me, and the rest of the vain silly fellows. The postmistress, now—what would *she* look like if she would have her own face made to order just as she wanted? Or the Minister? Or even your own Mother?—D'you see? What a—what a *dull* world it would be to walk about in! A lot of tailor's dummies! Not a single face worth looking at twice!—And so, too, that ideal book (or play, or film) someone somebody will make about Wales—the one all Welshmen will approve of, that fabulous book! No one will be able to read it, shall I tell you why? Because anyone who tries will fall into a beautiful, peaceful, deep, deep, sleep.

1951

ARLOTT ON DYLAN

John Arlott

I've always thought that of his kind he was the finest of all poetry readers. He really only had the one style, but that style stung the words out almost as if they were made of cut-glass. He was so sharp and so clear and he never did any poet less than justice. He didn't want to hurry through a poem, he wanted to give each word its full value, as he always did in his own poems, but so he did with other people's poems . . .

. . . The great thing was, of course, that as soon as he picked up a poem he looked at it and he understood it, and he was generous—no, he wasn't generous, he had a catholic taste over a wide, wide range of poems from the simplest to the most complex, but he detected and rejected the phoney absolutely on sight.

There he was with these sweaty ringlets hanging over his forehead and a dead cigarette hanging from his lower lip. It had always gone out and went up and down as he read and it was quite fascinating. Sometimes you could barely hear what he was saying for the fascination of seeing if the cigarette would fall.

He would hold the script with one hand and beat time with the other, and those big gooseberry eyes would be very wide, wide open, and he'd enter right into the soul of what he was reading. He used to entrance people more than I think anybody else I've ever listened to. When you were listening to him or watching him it was a quite irresistible urge to say: "Wonderful. Go on, don't stop." . . .

. . . Dylan broadcast for me for over six years and in that entire time he was never for one half minute drunk. He always arrived sober and these were long sessions. I mean, we ran from nine in the morning until half-past-five in the afternoon before we recorded.

I can't say he didn't have a drink afterwards; I don't say

161

we didn't both have a drink afterwards; I don't say a lot of us didn't have a drink afterwards, but he might have a pint of beer and a sandwich at lunchtime and he'd be back after lunch perhaps quicker than some of the others . . .

. . . I worshipped Dylan, I thought he was a great poet and a great reader. I thought he was a lovely man and when he died, I wept. Those years of the fall, when he was hard up, every farthing he ever borrowed off me he paid back and no cheque he ever drew me bounced.

I had a letter from him not long before the end saying: "Dear John, I need a lot of money. I don't want it all from you, I was going to say twenty pounds but send me ten pounds. I'm not going to promise to pay it back because I never shall and if you don't want to send it you needn't."

Thank God I sent it. It's the last time I ever heard from him, and if ever I thought a man had a touch of divinity it was Dylan.

1983

TWO MEN

Philip Burton

There were two contradictory Dylans. The one that the world knew, the show-off, the performer, the drunk; and there was the poet. That performer, that show-off, could never have written his tremendous poems. I think he's a truly, truly great poet but when you got him alone and he was discussing his work with you he was a very very different man.

I remember once we were in the Cafe Royal in London talking about what ultimately became *Under Milk Wood*—at that time I think it was tentatively called something like *The Village of the Damned.* Out of that came *Under Milk Wood* ultimately. He wanted me to do it, but by that time I was no longer in the BBC and couldn't.

We were having a wonderful conversation and then suddenly a third person appeared—I've forgotten who it was now but he was quite well known—and Dylan changed immediately. He became the show-off, the wisecracker, the entertainer, incredibly different. Dylan alone was one thing, Dylan in company was a very, very different person. Unfortunately that's the one that's got all the publicity. All that really matters is his poetry.

1983

THE VITAL WORD

Douglas Cleverdon

He was a very meticulous worker in the studio and I've even known him leave *The George* during lunch in order to go back to the studio in order to work on his part before the rest of the cast got back at half-past-two. He was very conscientious on anything that was concerned with words or poetry.

Everything else didn't matter, of course. I mean bills, money, appointments, they were of no importance whatever compared with the word, but when it was the matter of the word then he was as conscientious as a bank clerk.

1983

ANOTHER DYLAN

KINGSLEY AMIS

Kingsley Amis's novel, 'The Old Devils' won the Booker Prize in 1986. A central character in it is the dead, boozing, boyo of a poet. Brydan. He is a Dylan Thomas figure in the thinnest of disguises.

My chap Brydan—with no surname—is an even more decrepit equivalent of Dylan Thomas. As one of the characters says, it's made it impossible to write honestly or directly about Wales or anything else. Somehow the centre of attention is no longer the place and the people, it's the writer himself. It's an egotistical way of writing in which the reader's attention is drawn all the time to the cleverness of the writer and not to the quality of the material he's writing about . . .

Dylan Thomas—in so far as one can tell this sort of thing—was a writer of enormous natural talent—whatever that means—and I think he perverted it. It's a perilous thing to say and a very arrogant thing to say but I think his view of what poetry is and ought to be doing was a dangerous one; in a way, a ridiculous one. He tried to reduce everything to words on the page and, as far as possible, to forget what they meant or what they meant outside poetry.

It's a very sad thing. By some defect of temperament or maturity, of a way of growing up or not growing up, he made the worst use of what he really had.

1987

POETRY OF MEANING

GLYN JONES

Poetry, we've heard many times, is a matter of words, not a matter of ideas. We know of the obsession of many poets with words, of Whitman collecting words even off the advertisements on medicine bottles, of Browning's apprenticeship to poetry which included a careful reading of Dr. Johnson's dictionary. W. H. Auden says that if he heard of two young men, one eager to express great truths in his verse, and the other interested more in playing about with words in a sort of game, he would back the second of these as the one most likely to turn into a poet. Let us accept that poetry is a matter of words, not of ideas.

One of the snags about this is that words *themselves*, are in a sense ideas; speech and expression are so intimately bound up with the human psyche that this is so. Words cannot be treated as independent entities. As far as I know no successful poem has yet been composed with what Rossetti calls "stunning words" alone. Each word we use belongs in some intellectual or emotional context, and if it is torn out of that context and placed alongside other words similarly treated, the whole structure entirely loses significance.

Words, however jewel-like they may seem to us from time to time, simply cannot be treated as jewels and arranged in arbitrary patterns. The patterns, to achieve the effect of art, must have human validity and meaning. It's true that poetry often results from straining words away from the centre, to the edge of their context, as it were; the conjunction of words, each moved to an unusual position, can be aesthetically explosive. But a line of striking words all torn out and placed together becomes meaningless, intellectually and emotionally. Words remain stubbornly determined to *mean* something.

Poetry, in this way, is not only the stuff of ecstasy, it is also, because it uses words, deeply rooted in ordinary human experience; and abstract poetry, so often attempted, seems to me an impossibility. A poem must be involved in saying *something*, however trite and commonplace that something, reduced to prose terms, might be. Let us take, as an example of what I mean, a well-known poem—Dylan Thomas's *Fern Hill*. This poem seems in some ways to come very near to being pure, or abstract, poetry. It has no message, it advocates nothing, it doesn't stand for anything as against anything else, it criticises nothing, it tells no story, it works out no intellectual concept. It approaches the condition of music in being a paean of praise in celebration of a lost innocence. But it is, nevertheless, poetry and not music—poetry colourful and strongly pictorial. Every word in it has its own ambience. It must surely mean more to us if we understand what innocence is, and lost innocence. Dylan Thomas was able to write it because he was obsessed by words and obsessed also by innocence.

1966

SELECTED POEMS

John Ormond

A sense of time passing has always been one of the perennial fertile springs of poetry but you get to feel that it's rubbing it in a bit much when your work appears in anthologies with your name followed by brackets giving your date of birth followed by a dash and then a space leaving room for the book's owner to fill in the year of your death in due course. A nasty little blank hole to look into I can tell you. Born 1923—was it that long ago? 'I look into my glass and view my wasting skin' says Thomas Hardy in what I always call his Shaving Poem. Robert

Graves has one too. I've even written one myself which I call *As it Happens*.

> The ones whose images came unbidden
> Into me, brow, jaw-line and shoulder-stoop,
> Whose faces I shave daily; the long-hidden
> Similarities seen more surely later, the whole crop:
>
> I have them and take them all, having no choice,
> If not exactly gladly, vaguely seeing
> The sediments of my bedrock there to be rejoiced in,
> There being no alternative to being.

That's not a thought that used to haunt me but as I've got older it has rather. That the alternative to having the joys and the sorrows of one's life would have been not to have had them, never to have been born and, of course, if you pursue that notion it leads to the idea that the whole of life and the world and everything in space is one boundless miracle.

In the first introductory poem to my new book—I call it *The Gift*—I abandon hopes of trying to fathom the mystery.

> From where, from whom? Why ask, in torment
> All life long when, while we live, we live in it?
> As pointless to ask for truth in epiphanies
> That throb in the fire, rustle, then fall into ash;
> Or why stars are not black in a white firmament.
> Enough that it was given, green, as of right, when,
> Equally possible, nothing might ever have been.

More and more over the years I've found myself agreeing with Louis MacNeice that poetry is a precision instrument for recording a man's reactions to life and with Robert Frost who said "Poetry may be defined as a way of remembering what it would impoverish us to forget."

Also the poems in my book are much longer than the ones I've quoted. From among the elegies and the love poems and the celebratory poems, let me take one—again quite short—which describes the scene at the day's end when the swifts swoop by the thousand over the roofs of a small square in a little hill city in Tuscany. It's called simply, *Evening in the Square*.

> The swifts are invisibly mending the sky
> Where last night's wind tore it to pieces,
> Stitching, delirious with light labour,
> High on it, with dizzy double-darning
> Done in twos. Such work's a tall order.
>
> Clearly up there everything is still in tatters,
> Total anarchy, a right old tangle,
> All in each other's way. This lot need better
> Management, a good union. But they are natural
> Non-joiners, although they're fellow-travellers.
>
> Darker. They're frantic with deadline screeches.
> They'll never finish. The pigeons line
> The high eaves, baffled. Get an agent for this show,
> Do it with ribbons: a fortune. I'd do it myself
> But mine is, alas, only a poet's licence.

I'm getting older. I pray that every year the licence will be renewed so that yet again I'll get through my poetic MOT test, one careful owner, only used for going to the Muse's Church.

1987

A PAINTER'S CREED

NICHOLAS EVANS

The common people are with me, although I paint Jesus. I paint Him, I painted the Last Supper, I've painted Him going to the Cross, I've painted Him on the Cross but all the time the miner has been coming through; the common people.

Jesus, I believe, doesn't want so many pictures of himself on the walls or in stained windows, but he wants to come into our heart, not something without us, and it's the common man, the common clay, shall I say, should be moulded as objects of perfection.

1982

AGAINST THE MEGAPHONE

HYWEL DAVIES

The regional job, I believe, is much more than the winning of large audiences for such programmes in the 'prime time' of early morning radio and early evening television. Nor can the regions pretend, however attractive the insidious argument of decentralization might appear to be, however sensible and profitable the arrangement, that they are fulfilling their obligations by becoming editorially responsible for specialized programmes—industry in the North, natural history in the West, farming in the Midlands. Regional broadcasting is more than a newspaper and regional centres are more than 'studios of convenience'.

Or are they? Is this merely the fervour of a regional man? Is this not perhaps a regional searching for a star part, instead of a modest supporting role in the pattern of British broadcasting? Can any region today, with its limited resources, produce work which is professional

169

enough to stand without apology side by side with the best of Britain and America? Can a region say anything of truly entertaining and artistic value, apart from its coverage of news and current affairs, and should it try to do so when the job can obviously be done so much more easily from the metropolis? After all, we are a very small compact island and our several regional talents are not likely to be overlooked by London.

It all depends on the nature of the act of communication. If the BBC is a loudspeaker addressing the nation from afar, well and good. If the BBC is a means of mass communication addressing masses, well and good. If the BBC is a service in competition with commercial services, fighting for mass listening and viewing figures, well and good.

But we know well that the BBC is more than the sum of these parts. We know it to be a unique public service corporation, admired abroad if not at home, obligated from the beginning to root itself in the subsoil of its own community. It may not have gone deeply enough for people to feel without thinking that the BBC was 'Us' not 'Them'; but that, without doubt, was the aim.

If this is true, the BBC cannot exist without strong regional support and I can return, therefore, to my fervour. I repeat, regional centres must be more than studios of convenience. They should bear the names of Broadcasting House and Television Centre with the same awareness and pride as their great counterparts in London. They have the same right and the same require-ment to be a debating chamber, an exhibition centre, a publishing house, a theatre, a concert hall, a workshop. This is why the original arrangement of regions is still a necessary one, despite the adaptations and comprises already mentioned. A focal point, a centre, is better when it is near; and London, in this sense, can be too distant and alien a metropolis. This nearness, this ready avail-

P H BURTON

BBC Broadcasting House London W1

HYWEL DAVIES
BBC Broadcasting House London W1

ability, nurtures and develops the regional sense of identity.

The fundamental obligations of a region, in short, are deeper towards its community than towards its central organization. So the regional centre must proclaim its existence; it must state forthrightly its interest and involvement. And this is why, along the years, the regions —apart from paying constant attention to established cultural events—have earned a high reputation for their direct patronage of the arts, for their encouragement and support of playwrights, poets, and composers.

There are some amongst us who argue that our patronage has been too obvious and selfish an exercise. 'It's our job,' they say, 'to broadcast fresh music and new plays. Don't let's talk smugly about patronage when all we're really doing is making sure that we've got grist for our mill.' They argue forcibly that some worthwhile form of corporate activity, a large or small project that aims at bettering the community, deserves similar patronage, even to the extent of initiating a project, and that its final description in the shape of a programme is a proper exercise in broadcasting. I think the philosophy is sound because it demands a positive attitude towards the society served, a progressiveness, a good kind of editorial-izing and not mere reportage. I can think of nothing more disheartening and unrewarding than a broadcasting region which is characterized by retrospection and nostalgia, a kind of 'trust', a preserve for dying dodos. Broadcasting people should march, most of the time, in the vanguard of their society.

1965

APPRENTICESHIP

WYNFORD VAUGHAN-THOMAS

When Wynford Vaughan-Thomas came down from Oxford in 1930 he got a job giving talks to clubs for the unemployed in South Wales.

It was another world. There was I one moment in the rarified atmosphere of Oxford and the next there was I trying to sell myself to an unemployed club in Llansamlet. Never will I forget it. The organiser took me up for a trial lecture and there they were all crammed in a little hut with a stove.

In charge was one of the old-style union leaders. He was unemployed but he had it all completely organised and as soon as I delivered my halting address he said: "Well, boys, you've heard a marvellous address by a gifted man." That was the worst thing—I was only just beginning.

He said "All unanimous?"

Everybody voted yes.

"Mr. Thomas, you're in."

Then he saw Dai Bach was asleep at the stove. He said: "Wake Dai Bach up there and make it unanimous."

He turned to me and said: "Don't worry, Mr. Thomas, he's slept through a speech by Aneurin Bevan himself."

1983

In the 1930s, Wynford Vaughan-Thomas joined the BBC as an Outside Broadcast Assistant.

An Outside Broadcast Assistant did everything in those days. He did interviews, he did talks, he organised commentaries on events like rugby matches and TT trials and he, in fact, was right in the centre of the small station. It was a wonderful experience as everybody knew everyone and the towering figure of Sir John Reith, as he then was, Lord Reith, boomed over it all. A rather frightening man.

I'll never forget when I first joined. I walked towards him in his office and I thought he'd stood up to meet me. Not a bit of it. He was sitting down. Then he stood up higher and higher and higher, and he shook me by the hand.

He said: "Welcome aboard. Only one thing I'd like to tell you is this: never forget that the BBC is not an organ of mere entertainment."

And I never did.

1983

WINNING THE FRANCHISE

JOHN MORGAN

I had fallen-out with the BBC, very reluctantly, over the treatment of a film I had made in Vietnam. Two Senators had been flown-in from Washington to attack the film in the studio while I was at my wife's bedside in hospital. My film was true; moreover, my dismay at American behaviour was based on a love for America, a nation whose culture had shaped those of us brought up on the movies of the Forties, on its wits. Here was the emblem of freedom destroyed by its savagery. Since I had spent many months of my life explaining the inadequacies of life in communist societies, I didn't care for the kind of figures in the BBC who were suggesting that I was against American behaviour in Vietnam because I was left wing. One man who would have no part of that was Huw Wheldon. I told him I was going to leave and join colleagues who were departing from Panorama—Jeremy Isaacs, Philip Whitehead, Jolyon Wimhurst. He suggested that instead I might consider being Controller of the BBC in our home

173

country. It was a flattering suggestion but, I explained to Huw, I was congenitally incapable of having a job.

We then had the usual entertaining conversation in which he said I was quite wrong about him in a profile I'd done in the New Statesman suggesting he was interested in power. Nor me, I said.

What he had done, though, was put an idea in my mind. For ten years, apart from visits to parents and watching Wales play rugby, I'd hardly been to my own country. Within days I'd met old friends who had been at the BBC, all of whom were involved in organising bids for the franchises of independent television companies which were about to be renewed. Some were for Scotland, some for Yorkshire, some for the new London contracts. Mooching about in a state of some emotional confusion, with so much sickness in the family, and about the BBC and the New Statesman, I sat down with a piece of paper.

My method of work has always been a matter of fun to others. For some reason they find it hard to believe that staring at the sun, playing tennis, or working on a new drink, a list is being drawn up in the mind. Myself, I put it down to a combination of training in mathematical logic and air force organisation, that these lists are formulated. However, I have this document setting out what seemed to me necessary to seize the franchise for television in Wales and the West of England. My serious motive was that there should be a television station in Wales run for and by Welsh people. I had the idea that programme people should hold some sway. I wanted to try and preserve a spirit which had meant so much to my life in my own early, exuberant days. I wanted, too, Wales to be a European country with comparable standards.

So, the battle plan drawn up, I rang first Richard Burton whom I knew, and Wynford Vaughan Thomas whom I did not. Wynford was in London and we met. With that enthusiasm I was at once to admire, he abandoned his other television enterprise. Wales was our country. I explained my plan. Richard was in the South of France, filming. I flew to see him. He was his usual generous self—indeed offered to pay for the whole enterprise until I explained that it was not that kind of thing, but more political. In the end, which I regret, it didn't do him much good being so kind to myself and those that followed, when all he was being was patriotic and generous. Not that he was very good when he and a friend lost to myself and his wife Elizabeth Taylor at snooker.

When I came back from seeing Richard, I then went to see Geraint Evans at Covent Garden and Stanley Baker on location in Hertfordshire, and was very pleased at winning their support. Wynford, meanwhile, following the order of battle, had gathered together some other Welsh people and through his friend, the late Martin Cadbury, a group of Bristol businessmen, known to none of us. Since no-one except myself had dreamed of applying for this franchise, they were all, Wynford reported, a little bewildered. I had, meanwhile, rung my friend Aled Vaughan at the BBC in Cardiff, asking if, were we to win, he would be in charge of programmes in Cardiff. To my delight, he agreed. My difficulty was that there was going to be a putsch in Greece and perhaps a war in Israel and my feet were itching.

Looking through my diary for that period which is very complete, I find it interesting that I was so right. I was very concerned that whatever happened, the programme -makers at TWW should not be affected. In fact we never intended, or offered, any criticism, of the people with the franchise. There is also a note of conversation with Wynford that he shouldn't bother with people with money, since, if we won, we wouldn't be short of that.

It was our main dispute, and my new pal was wrong. My view had been that we had to assert the quality of ideas and talent over the dead weight of money, but, unfortunately, the weaker brethren prevailed. I couldn't complain because I was in a twin dilemma. Would I take a job? No.

More than that, having written a draft application, I was away for a while when Wynford beguiled the ideal chairman to pull so disparate a group together, David, Lord Harlech.

So we went to the IBA and were interviewed by Lord Hill and his colleagues. Because our consortium had been formed so suddenly and late, TWW, I think, were not aware of us. Those friends of mine in the television and press trades who knew, thought it was just another of my aphorisms: 'Nothing so composes the mind of a morning as to invent a television company'. The transcript is revealing. The chat is dominated by Lord Hill interrogating; the answers largely are by Lord Harlech, Walter Hawkins, a formidable Bristolian, and myself. In his autobiography, Lord Hill proposes that our success was due to our programme ideas and he generously ascribes the prominent part to myself. Myself, I'd put it down to the general strategy. The victory certainly had an effect on the minds and pockets of those in control of independent television. The programme makers were not disturbed.

The history of our company the audience can judge and anyway I don't think it proper to talk about one's colleagues in public, especially since I hope to be around for a while. Aled Vaughan's contribution to the quality of television in Wales has certainly been quite extraordinary and has made the company admired in most countries, although he is inclined to point out that he has taken the heat of day while I've lain in the Wye Valley whistling. I have a reflection, though, which it is possible to offer.

I must be the first and probably last person to invent a successful television company and lose money by it. There was a moment when the company was formed when Geraint Evans and myself, a *pair* of innocents, noticed all these fellows investing—and we hadn't thought of it. Such patriots. Mind you, I said, I'd rather be like that.

1979

AN UNBIASED OBSERVER

G. V. WYNNE-JONES

Just after the war I was asked by a member of the BBC if I would like to try doing some commentary because they were looking for a commentator and I said not so-and-so likely. I really hadn't thought of myself as a broadcaster at all. A little later someone said: "Would you come into the stand from a committee box in Cardiff and do a bit of commentary onto an old 78 record then, a bit of closed-circuit commentary?"

I didn't know what a closed-circuit commentary was so I went into the stand—I wasn't bothered about it—and I did a quarter of an hour's commentary and promptly forgot about it.

A few weeks later I had a phone call to ask me if I'd go into the BBC in Park Place and listen to a recording which several other people had also done. So we sat down and they played a record. Then they played a second one and the chap next to me said: "What do you think of that?"

I said: "Not much."

He said: "Pity—that was me."

So I kept quiet then for a bit and about three or four further on another voice came on and I'd never heard my voice on record so like a fool I said: "That's the bloke."

And they said: "That's you." I will never, ever forget it.

1985

BEHIND THE ARRAS

RICHARD BURTON

I was playing Hamlet. It was, of course, a Saturday afternoon and that day we had a new boy playing for Wales called Lewis Jones, who later turned professional. I was on the stage and transistor radios had just come in; that is, if you were influential enough to get one. I had one and it was kept offstage. The entire cast from Ophelia to Polonius to Claudius to Gertrude to everybody had to come on the stage and, as they turned to face me, put up their hands and say how many points we were losing by or winning by.

I was terribly worried about that match and we won it by 11 points to 5 and Lewis Jones was the architect of the first try which was, of course, scored by the immortal, and lamentably now dead, Tubby Davies of Cardiff. I was very aware of that match and still feel, if you give me a couple of drinks, that I was actually there, though in actual fact I was having a go at Hamlet at the time.

1970

HEADLINES, LIBELS AND HANGINGS

Hugh Cudlipp

The three Cudlipp brothers all became editors of Fleet Street newspapers. Hugh—eventually Lord Cudlipp— became head of a huge newspaper empire, but he started in the trade for the most practical reasons.

The reason that my two brothers and I went into newspapers is that my elder brother Percy gained a certain amount of modest local fame as Cardiff's boy poet at the age of 12 or 13. He later became a reporter and I was very impressed with the fact that when he came home he was always handing out free tickets for the cinemas—and I thought that a profession which gave you free tickets for the cinemas was a very attractive one.

I'm quite sure that some people went into the written word for nobler reasons, but I must confess that the reason I went in was two tickets for *Me and My Girl* at the *Olympia* cinema in Queen Street, Cardiff.

His journalistic career began on a very odd South Wales newspaper.

It was called *The Penarth News*, and under its title it said 'with which is incorporated the *Glamorgan Gazette* and the *Dinas Powis Bugle*' or some name like that. Now none of these papers actually existed, but it made the Penarth News that much more important. Unfortunately the paper went bankrupt when I'd been on it for three months. But I had one great experience there—I was able to perform my first libel at the age of 14.

I was asked to cover a football match between Penarth and Barry. I knew nothing about football and the result of the match was 5—0 with Penarth losing. I noticed that the referee came from Barry and this struck me as very sinister. Quite clearly, had the referee come from Penarth instead of Barry I thought that Penarth might have won. I made the mistake of mentioning this notion in the newspaper, but we weren't sued for libel by the referee because he knew as much about libel as I knew about football.

I then went to a paper called the *Evening Express* in Cardiff and I worked for that for six months. Then, unfortunately, I was endeavouring to get my expenses passed when the editor—who had advanced information that the paper was amalgamating with another one—that night—endeavoured to commit suicide.

I didn't get my expenses passed but I was able to save this man by producing my boy scout knife from my belt and cutting the cord from which he was hanging behind a roll top desk in his office. When five o'clock came we all knew why he'd done it—he had no faith in the future.

However, he was a most pleasant person. I got a job in Manchester and when I came back to report this to my parents a month later, the first man I met in St. Mary Street was this editor. He said to me: "Well, Hugh, I'm glad to see you're looking very well, how are you?"

And I said, with some astonishment, having seen him last at an angle of 45 degrees behind his desk, "Well, how are *you*?"

1976

COMING BACK

Goronwy Rees

When Goronwy Rees returned from Oxford to Wales in 1953 to become Principal of the University College of Wales, Aberystwyth, he was clearly uneasy about the attitudes he would discover. His premonitions were justified when he found himself in the middle of a sensational public row. He was revealed as the source of a series of articles in The People *about the defectors Burgess and Maclean. The tumult that followed ended only when Rees resigned following a report by a committee of inquiry set up at the college.*

What is surprising is the permanence and persistence of the Welsh way of life and belief, an intense cultural and intellectual conservatism which shows itself sometimes in an almost Chinese reverence for what is established and sanctified by custom, a strange form of ancestor worship which is all the stranger because, as an articulate body of thought and belief, it is not more than a hundred and fifty years old. I would say quite sincerely, that the most striking single impression I have received on returning to Wales is that of the strangely rigid and unchanging habit of thought and belief of the Welsh people today.

It is not for me to say whether this is a good thing or a bad thing; it depends very largely on temperament whether we approve or mistrust an unshakeable loyalty to our native gods, even though sometimes the magic may seem to have gone out of them. I simply record an impression. Yet one cannot help contrasting the immense productiveness of the Welsh people in the nineteenth century in creating their own characteristically Welsh institutions, and what seems to me today to be an inability either to create new institutions or to adapt existing institutions to the changed conditions of the present time.

It may well be, of course, that in this the Welsh are no different from other Western peoples, that Western civilisation as a whole has become rigid and, from that point of view, self-destructive, in face of the amazing scientific and technological revolution in which we live—a revolution which affects modes of thought just as much as means of production. But it may be also that the Welsh have an additional difficulty to overcome in the struggle, in which we all share to some extent, to adapt ourselves to a new and revolutionary world.

1953

OVER THE DYKE

Glyn Roberts

Roughly speaking, I think you can divide the London Welsh into three principal groups. The first of these consists of what you might call the very successful and partially uprooted handful of men and women who have become so prominent and so absorbed in their professions that they've had to cut themselves off, to some extent, from purely Welsh circles. Among them, of course, you'll find business men, lawyers, doctors and surgeons, civil servants, architects, actors, artists, journalists, and creative writers. The second group is a very big one, the biggest of the three probably, and it's always been and still is the core of the organised Welsh communities in

London. It consists of, I should say, somewhere about a hundred thousand people drawn from nearly all the counties of Wales in about equal proportions. Nearly all of them speak Welsh, and speak it well and obstinately. By obstinately I mean that they won't forget it. They are religious, and provide the faithful and fervent congregations at upwards of twenty Welsh chapels in different parts of London.

Most of them are in business in a small way—either running their own little independent dairy, working in the drapery trade, or, in smaller numbers, in almost every form of commerce imaginable. They are conservative, conventional, upright people, who wear very orthodox clothes and set great store on respectability. The over-whelming majority of them look forward to saving enough money to enable them to return to Wales and settle down to a quiet, unruffled life in the villages in which they were born—and most of them do.

The third group and the newest consists of young men who have been driven up to London from industrial South Wales simply because there is no work for them in their own towns. As you know, there has been a very big expansion of industry in the south of England during the last ten years, and one of the results of this has been to create a demand for young, strong and adaptable labour. And South Wales was full of men who were young, strong and adaptable. All round London, new industrial towns sprouted like mushrooms—if you've ever entered London by road, you must have passed through several of them. Factories making motor-cars on a large scale, or in some cases assembling parts already made; scores of factories directly or indirectly bound up with the boom in aerial re-armament; literally thousands of small factories making various kinds of luxury products, health and beauty accessories, wireless gadgets and everything else that is modern. Boys from South Wales are working by tens of thousands in these places, side by side with men from farms in Ireland, from the coalfields of Lanark and the ship yards of the Clyde, from the mill towns of Lancashire and the steel centres of the north-east coast.

1938

OVER THE POND

EMRYS JONES

Broadcasting about the Welsh immigrants in Utica, New York State, in 1950, Emrys Jones examined the reasons for the rapid decline of the Welsh language and culture in the area.

The stream of Welsh ceased, more or less, in 1914, and within twenty or thirty years the change made itself felt—the chapels introduced English services for the first time, and the amount of Welsh written in *Y Drych* dropped rapidly. This doesn't mean that the Welsh were being Americanised for the first time. Each generation since the mid-nineteenth century had undergone that process, but this never became apparent. Newcomers from Wales filled their places. That was why the Welsh retained their language and customs, why the chapels flourished, why the Eisteddfod and the Gymanfa Ganu were noteworthy events. But the newcomers have ceased, and the process of change has revealed itself. There is no new generation to take the place of that which is rapidly dying out. In a decade or two there will be practically no Welsh-born Welshman in Utica, but several thousand Americans of Welsh origin.

Does this mean that the Welsh and their cultural contribution will disappear without a trace? No, not at all. Some traditions will continue in a changed form, because even the American Welsh are very proud of certain cultural traits, to which they have a sentimental attachment. The Welsh have made a considerable contribution. The Eisteddfod is a case in point. The annual Eisteddfod is approaching its centenary in this city, but it is no longer confined to the Welsh. Indeed, it has dropped most of the features, such as poetry and prose, which would limit it to Welsh-speaking people. It is now a Utican festival at which Italians, Poles and Germans carry away more prizes than the Welsh.

The word "Eisteddfod" is a sacred word, and will be retained, and all the organising is done by those of Welsh descent. But it has been adapted in content to meet a new situation—its preservation depended on that.

1950

COME OFF IT, MR. CHIPS

Gwyn Thomas

A school is unlike any other place of work. Its material is alive, crafty, defiant. Its handling techniques are mysteriously opaque when they are not delightedly stupid. We cannot know what in forty years from now will be the fruit or the doom of the sentences that fall, day in, day out, from our lips. Bemusedly, charitably, for all we know, we work as much cruelty in the psychological dark as Jack the Ripper did in the physical penumbra of Shoreditch. In self-defence, for we minister to a touchy, fierce, contemptuous tribe, we borrow from the priest, the witch-doctor and those curious artisans who worked the rack in ancient times. If the message of our collective drum through the silence and perplexity of a good many adult lives is not easily deciphered it is because the drummers had very little idea of what they wanted to say. It takes a very steady drumstick to withstand the tightly united staring of thirty astonished boys who have become suddenly aware that your clothes, notions, jokes, gestures

184

and grimaces have just at that instant dropped down dead in a world that is not yours in any real sense at all.

The average schoolboy is a kind of sexton-beetle. He is eager to slap his little pat of new life on the old and the alien. More lessons than one strike the precise note of a brisk funeral with this or that part of the pedagogue laid low never to rise again.

No one will, in fact, admit that this is so, and in fiction your Mr. Chips will transform the savage, sadistic impercipience of his charges into a vast outlet of affection. This is what gives the flavour of a quite terrifying comicality to teaching. If there is a cosmic jest, and with our kind of luck there probably is one, this will turn out to be its furthest frontier. I would, on balance, given a better eye and a stronger wrist, have preferred to be a wood-chopper. At least the blocks and faggots do not walk around with your traumas notched in decorative designs all over them.

1960

A VICTORIAN EDUCATION

Berta Ruck

My Victorian boarding-school was in Bangor, Caernarvonshire. My school-fellows were nearly all Welsh girls. Many of them talked only Welsh at home. Some of them produced clothes-lists with such curious items as "1 print frog" and "1 flannel pet-cat."

The mistresses were for the most part conscientious, bewildered English-women, who (or do I fancy this?) felt it as a mission to come to *these wilds* and teach the more or less friendly young aborigines with outlandish names like Myfanwy.

Our school was run on Spartan lines. Never, before or

since, have I endured cold so bitter as that of the top-floor dormitory misnamed *The Nest*.

One Christmas term when even Llanberis Lake was frozen over, we used to have to go to bed in bloomers and thick stockings, wearing, over our nightgowns, our outdoor coats. Young and tough, we took this with simple jokes about "arctic explorers" and "furthest north". We were allowed one warm bath a week. Otherwise we washed in icy water in basins on little iron tripods. Our food—except on Sundays when we were allowed to "pool" for tea the cakes and jam brought from home, our food was not much better than that of political prisoners. Healthily hungry, we wolfed everything set before us. Bread with golden-syrup soaked into doorstep slabs; rice pudding and treacle described by us as maggots and tar, other dishes known by school-names even less polite—all tasted to me equally delicious. For somehow that Spartan place was, unexpectedly "a happy ship", a gay school. I enjoyed the companionship of my Welsh school-fellows (some of them still write to me). I enjoyed the two-by-two country walks. And those Saturday afternoons, when I went out to tea with friends in the town. One clerical-literary family were, I now realise a "formative influence." The girl and boy around my own age exchanged with me plots of novels we'd read. (I was *told*—it may be a family legend!—that the boy could only be got to wash his neck when I was expected.) The delightful mother who, though English, spoke several languages fluently, including Welsh, had been made a Bard. The first I'd seen. She wore, appropriately, long green, "Liberty" dresses. Also the first I'd seen. At tea in her dining-room I gazed at a picture which gave me faith in Survival more surely than anything I was taught at school. It was a slightly scaring, but fascinating print by William Blake. *The Soul Revisits The Body After Death.* My reaction: "Why, of course it does! looking like that, too."

1957

ON THE BEACH

Susan Cooper

We fought formal down on the beach by a breakwater, under the towering slime-green timber legs of the jetty when the tide was out; one gang on the beach itself, the other across rocks slippery with squelching popping wet bundles of seaweed, on a shoal of the shifting sands of the Dovey. It was a battle at a distance, fought by hurling sand-balls for which we had a Welsh name which I have forgotten. You scooped up a piled handful of wet sand, wet enough but not too wet or it would disintegrate; you moulded it into a perfect ball with both your hands, and then you rolled it lightly in the dry silvery sand higher up—not I think for any practical purpose, but only for the flourishing finish of the craftsman.

I made these, proudly, hastily, my heart hot in my throat with excitement, and thrust them into the badly outstretched hands of the warriors, the bigger boys with a deadly eye and a strong throw. And sometimes, stooping down, I would stagger as one hurled from the other side hit the top of my head, and with my face splattered with sand I would feel prouder still; a blooded warrior, even if I was, really, only the woman reloading the guns.

These battles always ended one way, with a stone slyly or accidentally thrown in the centre of one of the sand-balls, and a howl of pain and a silent unconscious figure on the other side. And if our gang were the offenders we would run wildly away in sudden hushed panic; but somehow no-one ever came to any harm, and half-realising this we would forget about the "accident" before we were halfway down the street.

1957

PRISON

MERFYN TURNER

In a way I suppose I was born to go to prison. That is, I don't remember ever deciding that I would be a pacifist. Welsh, nonconformist upbringing, my environment, my childhood heroes, made me into a pacifist as naturally, I hope, as different forces and factors shape others for a career in the Armed Forces. I was nurtured on men like Martin Luther, John Bunyan, the Quaker Fathers, and the nineteenth century Reformers. They weren't all pacifists by any means. But they were men of integrity, and inflexibility of purpose and belief. And then I had the great privilege to learn from men like my own uncle, Gwynfryn Jones, and George M. Ll. Davies. T. E. Nicholas, and John Morgan, Ystumtuen. To know them was to want to be like them, for each one was a saint in his own right.

I thought I was prepared for prison. I had read books and pamphlets, and I thought I knew all there was to know. But emotionally I was a sitting target. When those massive wooden gates cracked open and I stood before the steel gates which stood silent and sinister, and a voice called out of the gloom, "Another bloody reception," I began to feel sick, and a little lonely. And when I'd been stripped of my own clothes and dressed in my prison outfit, drab, shapeless, impersonal, and I'd had my medical examination—that is, the vet, as they called the doctor, had asked me if I was all right—and I'd been marched to my cell, and for the first time in my life been locked up, I felt as if all the world had abandoned me.

Like all men who stand in the dock, and then face the shock of the first time in prison, I slept little that first night. The Magistrates who sentenced me must have thought I was a particularly hard case, for they added Hard Labour to my sentence. That meant I had to sleep on a wooden bed-board. But it wasn't merely the physical discomfort that kept we awake so much as the fear of the unknown.

There might have been a couple of hundred men in the cells around me. But I couldn't hear a sound even from my nearest neighbour. I was alone, and all I could hear was the occasional padding of the night guards as they made their rounds, and the wild beating of my own heart. That night was long, and the stillness frightening. In the darkness I washed and dressed. I sat on my bed-board, and waited. And then confusion. A bell shattered the silence. Gas-lights sprang to life. Keys grated in locks. My cell door swung open. "Slop out! Shut your mouths! Get back to your cells and shut your doors!" Men were running around the landings, full pots in one hand, empty water jugs in the other. I joined the mad rush. When I reached the recess the floor was already awash, and the stench was abominable. I took a deep breath, aimed the contents in the direction of the lavatory pan, and scurried back to my cell.

I've been going in and out of prison pretty regularly for the last fourteen years, and many prisoners have told me, "Prison doesn't hurt me at all. I can do this bit of bird—as imprisonment is known in the trade—on my head." Then I tell them not to talk nonsense. Prison was meant to hurt, and though physical conditions change, nobody comes out of prison unscathed. Loss of freedom is in itself punishment. But there's separation too, and segregation, and the humiliation of a lost identity. For everything about prison strips a man naked of all that makes him different from a hundred others.

That hurt me every day of my sentence, hurt me more by far than the long, weary, idle hours I spent in my cell—eighteen on week-days, and twenty-two on Sundays: conditions, by the way, that are unchanged today for many thousands of prisoners. It hurt me more than the hunger for food and tobacco that tormented me until I found myself bartering for a few extras, and breaking the prison rules with not as much as a twinge of conscience.

You see, prison degrades the man. You may go in with high principles. But unless you belong to the saints, you leave those principles at the Gate, and collect them again as you leave when your sentence is done. The code of conduct you use while you are inside is the code dictated by your fellow prisoners. It is a code of survival, and the devil take the hindmost.

1960

CONVERSATION WITH STALIN

GEORGE THOMAS, LORD TONYPANDY

In 1947, George Thomas, the M.P. for Cardiff Central, was a member of a Labour party group visiting Czechoslovakia, Yugoslavia, Poland and the USSR. In Moscow they met the Soviet Foreign Minister, Mr. Molotov, who had a surprising proposition for them.

As we were taking our leave of Molotov we had a surprise, for he suddenly said "I know that you gentlemen would like to see Comrade Stalin, but he is away from Moscow." We said we had given up hope of seeing the great man, and the Molotov astonished us by offering to put a plane at our disposal, so that we could fly next morning to Stalin's home on the Black Sea. We did what you would have done; we accepted with pleasure and next day we flew 1,000 miles to the Black Sea (which, by the way, is blue). After touching down, we followed a long winding road from the airport to Marshal Stalin's villa, which is no more pretentious than a bank manager's house in this country. I kept a keen eye open for the armed guards I expected to find along the road, but only when we reached the very gate did I see two soldiers on duty. We knocked, and someone inside opened a peephole in the door—at which an irreverent demon whispered in my ear: "Knock three times and ask for Joe!"

Stalin received us in his study. I was interested to note that there was not a single picture on the walls of his room. Appropriately enough, the walls were a red mahogany, and there was a red mahogany desk. Mr. Stalin was dressed in a slate grey suit without decoration of any sort. He was wearing a pair of riding boots just like an English country gentleman. Throughout our talk he smoked his pipe.

Stalin looked to me like an ageing man who is rather feeling the strain of his responsibilities. He looked about 70, though I believe he is actually in the middle sixties.

But, in the course of the conversation, he revealed that his mind is keen and alert: he was both shrewd and quick in sizing up any problem we raised.

The first question we discussed was whether Russia really meant to co-operate with the Western powers, because, we said, there are many people who believe the Soviet Union wants to concentrate on her own internal problems for the next few years. If so, it would be a waste of time to try and establish better relations with her. Stalin said emphatically—and I quote him—"Undoubtedly the Soviet Union wants to co-operate. The same talk about isolation was also heard after the First World War and at one time it did even become possible to isolate the Soviet Union. Later diplomatic relations had to be established with her and during the Second World War even a Treaty of Alliance."

Then he went on to say, "Soviet people are not afraid of isolation. They are used to such talk." He went on to say that unless Socialists had enough foresight to take the initiative in Europe, the Communists would rally around them all the democratic forces. I interrupted to say "Thank you for the warning", and he at once replied

"You're welcome." We all burst out laughing. The very last words of Stalin to us were these: "The workers of Great Britain and the Soviet Union will always remain friends."

Undoubtedly many of you who are listening to me will marvel at the duality in Soviet policy, for at the very time when Molotov and Stalin were speaking such warm and kindly words to us, the Russian radio was uttering in withering terms a denunciation of the policy of our Government. I can't pretend to be able to interpret the reasons for this apparently contradictory policy which the Soviet Union is pursuing, but I do feel at least that the more contacts there are between our two peoples, the more chance there is of an ultimate understanding.

1947

LAWRENCE OF OXFORD

A. G. PRYS-JONES

T. E. Lawrence was my senior by one year as an undergraduate of Jesus College, Oxford. We were both reading for the same Final Honours School, that of Modern History. I met him for the first time in the Christmas Term of 1908, in the rooms of a friend who had been at the Oxford High School with him. I took an instinctive liking to Lawrence. He was that type of man. You either took to him at once, or you had considerable doubts about him.

For the two hours he was there, that late afternoon, he said extremely little, but sat cross-legged on a cushion on the floor, listening to our conversation, and rocking himself almost imperceptibly to and fro, frequently smiling in that Mona Lisa manner which I found was so characteristic of him. I remember wondering what was going on inside his mind, and suddenly it occurred to me that he was laughing at us. I said to my friend, "Lawrence has got some huge private joke of his own on. Why doesn't he give us the clue so that we can all laugh?"

To this Lawrence replied "Everything amuses me. You mustn't take me too seriously." "This is a quaint customer," I thought. But as I had always had a leaning towards rebels and people who didn't conform to the normal cut, I suggested, before he left, that he should come along and see me sometime.

He did, very soon, and again he sat cross-legged on the floor quietly explaining that he never sat on chairs if he could help it, that he never indulged in the meals known as breakfast, lunch, tea and dinner, nor smoked nor took drinks; in fact that he did nothing which qualified him to be an ordinary member of society. But, he added drolly, that he had no objection whatsoever to my doing any of those things, if I took the same broad view regarding his own abstentions.

At this first private meeting I found conversation a bit difficult. Lawrence was either too shy or too absorbed in his own private jokes and meditations to say much. But when he *did* speak, his comments were pithy, pungent and humorous; indicating that his interests were extremely wide and out of the ordinary, and that his capacity for reading was immense. He went away as quietly as he came in, almost timorously, thanking me most politely for having harboured him.

Within a minute or two after he had left, a very normal, intimate friend of mine dropped in. He was a typical rowing and rugger man of the old school, and of the old school tie, a stalwart upholder of tradition and correctness in all things, superlatively honest, dependable and loyal. In his blunt Anglo-Saxon way he said, "I've just passed that lunatic Lawrence on the staircase. What's he been doing in our territory?"

"Seeing me," I replied.

"My God, Tim, the man's barmy. Don't you know that?"

"Well," I said. "Either that or some kind of a genius. I can't tell yet. Give me time, old man; I've only just recently met him."

"You Welshmen do seem to have the knack of picking up the queerest fish. I know he's barmy. He doesn't run with the boats, he doesn't play anything. He just messes about on an awful drop-handled bicycle. And if he ever wore a bowler hat he'd wear it with brown boots."

"Well, well," I said, "that of course is perfectly dreadful: but he's got the most charming manners, probably a first-class brain, and he's most refreshingly out of the ordinary." But he replied "He'll always be plain barmy to me."

1946

INVESTITURE

Sir Harry Luke

In 1969, shortly before the investiture of the Prince of Wales at Caernarvon Castle, Sir Harry Luke described the first such ceremony—held in July 1911.

I attended the ceremony with my Oxford friend, Harry Pirie-Gordon, through the good offices of whose father, a Breconshire landowner, we were allotted excellent seats in the Outer Bailey. From these we had a perfect view of the actual investiture of the Prince by the King; this involved putting upon him the mantle, sword, coronet, ring, and "golden verge" or sceptre. Coronet and ring were made of gold mined in Wales. Then came the touching spectacle of the Prince being raised from his knees and kissed by his father on both cheeks in the sight of all the people. The new King and Prince then pass behind the Dais to Queen Elinor's Gate, and next beneath the heavy gothic mouldings of the King's Gate. Here, framed in its arch, and with the sun burnishing the Prince's golden hair and crown and his robes of purple and ermine, the King presented his son to the thousands of Welshmen outside to a veritable thunder of cheers.

When the Prince had previously made his separate entry before being invested, he was bareheaded and dressed at that stage in white silk knee-breeches and purple ermine-trimmed surcoat. When, in due course, he advanced between his supporters, Lords Plymouth and Kenyon, to the Royal Dais to be invested, girded, robed and crowned, he seemed a youthful Prince Charming from some fairy-tale of the Middle Ages. Many years later, in his autobiography, "A King's Story", the Duke of Windsor has referred to this dress as "a fantastic costume" and "a preposterous rig."

To a shy, modest, diffident young midshipman of 17, unable to see himself and very likely conscious of possible gunroom leg-pulling to come, this may well have been a comprehensible reaction. But I should doubt very much if it was the impression his ceremonial apparel as the invested Prince of Wales made on a single one of the spectators. To them, at that moment, he was without question the incarnation of all the fairy princes who have ever been imagined.

1969

195

TRADITION v HISTORY

Gwyn A. Williams

What defined the Welsh in the end were the English. In the open lowlands a strong, unifying monarchy emerged early, to become almost unique in the Europe of its day and to be strengthened still further by the injection of Norman power in the eleventh century. The relatively rapid rise of a powerful England turned the Welsh, almost from birth, penned as they were in a harshly poor upland economy staked to a bony mountain spine, into a marginal people. Talented but marginal, the talent probably a function of the marginality, light of foot, light of spirit, light of plough, they lived by their wits, the Jews of the British Isles.

The Welsh as the English called them, succumbing early to their deplorable national habit of addressing natives as foreigners, the Cymry, as about half of them called themselves, emerge into history from the wreck of Roman Britain as highly self-conscious heirs of the British. There was a profound divergence between the historical experience of north and south, possibly the root cause of their divergence in language. The romanised Commonwealth of the Silures generated a kingdom of Gwent-Morganwg, heavily Roman in its style and climate, living close to Celts in the south-west and Brittany, who were excluded from the Cymry who defined themselves in battle in north Britain. Ringed by immigrant kingdoms of Irish origin fusing, largely through the David evangelical style of Christianity into the ramshackle confederation of Deheubarth, Gwent-Morganwg, for centuries an extension of the civilisation of Salisbury Plain, seems to have settled relatively easily behind the Wye even as Gwynedd, under its north British dynasty of Cunedda, defined itself in the struggle for North Britain before falling apart in the eighth century as

Powys emerged as the survivor kingdom of an extensive Romano-British polity on the Severn.

Hardly had these piratical little kingdoms defined themselves as British and Christian than the internal breakdown of their inherited Roman super-structure coincided with a need to reshape settlement and tenurial patterns in the teeth of a voraciously land-hungry church at the very moment when the terrible scourge of the Vikings broke on them, to drive their new High Kings of all Wales generated by this internal crisis into the shelter of the new English Crown focused on Wessex. In a battle of the traditions, the old British ideology of Nennius and *Armes Prydein* against the new Britain of Hywel Dda in which the Welsh were a junior partner, Welsh social structure and polity were shaped by Hywel's Laws in political dependence on the English Crown, even as many Welsh princelings became half-Vikings themselves within the cultural world of the Irish Sea, that mini-Mediterranean of the north.

Hard on the heels of English and Vikings, came the Normans who ripped half the country away into a rich and hybrid Welsh-European civilisation, projected Welsh culture into Europe, thrust European modes into the semi-independent west and north and dragged the Welsh out of the Celtic-Scandinavian world into the Latin. In response, the Welsh around the survivor kingdom of Gwynedd struggled to build a miniature Welsh feudal state, to win a brief success under Llywelyn ap Gruffydd, first and last Welsh prince of Wales, who was broken by armies largely Welsh in composition and by a Welsh aristocracy in revolt against Llywelyn's ruthless abrogation of Welsh tradition, marshalled by Edward I who revolutionised English society in order to destroy Gwynedd. The colonial centuries which followed were ended by the Rebellion of Owain Glyn Dŵr, a war of national liberation which like all such wars was also the greatest of Welsh civil wars, to be followed by the seminal

197

Tudor century, when the Welsh gentry climbed to power over the ruins of principality and aristocracy alike, when the Welsh were hoisted to a temporary pinnacle of prestige, when the old British ideology of the Welsh became a new British national mythology and when Welsh society was absorbed wholesale into English.

That century witnessed that characteristic Tudor contradiction, a Protestant Welsh Bible to direct and service the survival of the old language on the one hand, official discrimination against and social scorn for that language on the other. Even as the old culture stammered before the Renaissance as Protestantism rooted itself in Welsh soil, the long and rich tradition of Welsh writing in the English language was born as the Welsh language began its slow recession into a sacerdotal tongue, a sacred language, and lost contact with the fullness of modern secular living.

The century of turmoil which followed the Tudors decimated the lesser gentry of Wales, a product of its kindred social structure and critical to its separate identity, and expelled it from public life, even as its land-owners were clasped into the hot and clammy embrace of the broad, open, astute and ruthless oligarchy of the new Great Britain and its unprecedented mercantile empire of the eighteenth century.

The alternative society in Wales was born no less of that new mercantile Britain with its Atlantic dimension: an evangelical drive for literacy which turned a majority of the adult population technically literate in Welsh for a stretch of the eighteenth century, a Calvinistic Methodist movement independent in its origins from English Methodism, stirrings of rationalist and radical movements among the Old Dissent created by embattled Puritanism and an upsurge of interest in Welsh history and antiquities powered above all by the London-Welsh, surrogate capital of an invertebrate country.

The entry of this alternative society into history was explosive. From the eighteenth century, the new industrial capitalism thrust into Wales. Over a hundred years it quintupled the population, sucked most of it into the modernising and English-speaking south-east, provided the money and the power and the will for a Welsh revival and the insidious processes which cut that revival down in its prime.

Over little more than two generations, the Welsh went on their Long March out of Establishment and into the spiritual world of Dissent, even as south and east began theirs into West Britain.

A further surge of growth built south Wales into an imperial metropolis of the new British world economy even as, in response, a new and semi-political Welsh nation clawed its way into half-existence, displacing and dismissing into limbo the half-formed Jacobin nation of the 1790s, to form along a language line and a religious line which was also a class line, to claim a monopoly of Welshness in the late nineteenth century even as a new industrial civilisation blossomed in the imperial democracy of south Wales and there was a massive, buoyant and innovatory immigration into that south Wales second in intensity only to immigration into the USA itself. And after a Klondyke climax to this new American Wales in the First World War, the terrible Depression of the 1920s and 1930s burned through this complex and contradictory Wales like radioactive fall-out from a distant holocaust.

The Depression which plays the same social role in Welsh history, I think, as the Famine in Irish, unhinged this Welsh polity, devastated its communities, dispersed a quarter of its people and thrust a community of survivors, struggling to rebuild consensus in a precarious post-war prosperity into those crises of identity and those bankruptcies of rooted political traditions which plague our contemporary experience.

In such a people with such a history, the problem of identity has been desparate from the beginning. In recent centuries we have progressively lost our grip on our own past. Our history has been a history to induce schizophrenia and to enforce loss of memory. Professional history, history as a craft, is even more recent a phenomenon in Wales than in England. Half-memories, folklore, traditions, myths, fantasy are rampant. We are a people with plenty of traditions but no historical memory. We have no historical autonomy. We live in the interstices of other people's history.

1979